DLB

DADDY'S LITTLE BOY

A journey to finding your true identity in Christ

VINCE MERCARDANTE SR., DLB

CrossHouse Publishing
2844 S. FM 549
Suite A
Rockwall, TX 75032
www.crosshousebooks.com

ISBN: 978-1-61315-015-3
Library of Congress: 2011937981

2

One of my greatest loves in this life is to be able to sit out in my Carolina Room, which has a beautiful view of the Inlet Waterway, while I hold a hot drink and a good book.

But often my life is like that of everyone else's in ministry—I allow the busyness of my days to steal this great love away. So when I do get those moments to enjoy this lost art, I am very picky about the books I read. I want to read to either relax, to learn, or to be exhorted. I have experienced all of these situations as I read Vince Mercardante's new book, *DLB: Daddy's Little Boy*.

For years my husband, Jack, and I have known Vince and his wife, Rose. I remember we first saw them during a season of desperation in their lives and in their relationship. Since both were performance-driven pastors, we could sense the "Just-tell-us-how-to-fix-it" or the "Tell-us-what-to-do-to-make-it-better" flowing from their souls. So we took them on a boat ride on a beautiful lake in upstate South Carolina. I think they thought that eventually they would get that (how-to-fix-it) list, but instead all we had to offer them was our experience and an impartation of a love for which one did not have to perform—an impartation of a love that had brought so much healing in our own lives and family that now it was touching the world.

They wanted this experience not to elude them any longer. They sought the missing link of knowing that they are loved and have a place of value in a relationship with a loving Father.

This revelation has been stolen from so many of us. So many of us have lost the ability to believe that our Father God is a loving, kind Father and that He loves us, period. No amount of performing will ever cause us to enter into a secure belief that we have purpose and destiny. Only when we become desperate and start searching for Him will we find the healing we need.

In this book *DLB: Daddy's Little Boy* Vince shares his experiences while he also helps the reader to understand no 10-step program to this revelation of love is available. Entering into that place of knowing we are Daddy's Little Boy or Girl arrives from a position of rest and not striving.

I am honored to recommend this book to all of you who have searched and still do not quite get this whole intimacy thing with a loving Father.

In their journey Vince and Rose are honest, real, and very transparent. If you truly want to discover your place in the Father's heart, then I challenge you to find the courage to read this book, to pray, and to allow the Holy Spirit to uncover your pain that might hinder you from discovering your destiny.

This book is enticing to the reader because it is real and offers you a challenge to become all that you have been created to be: to discover your destiny. Ralph Waldo Emerson sums up the choices that this couple has made: Don't go where the path may lead but instead go to where there is not a path and blaze a trail.

This book blazes that trail of openness and honesty that will take you into the belief that you, too, are Daddy's Little Boy or Girl.

Patricia Frost
Co-Founder/President
Shiloh Place Ministries

I dedicate this book to the memory of three people whose lives have made such a tremendous impression on my life.

First, I dedicate this book to my mom, **Nancy A. Mercardante**, who died on January 9, 2000. Without her there, I would have missed so much in life. I am so thankful to the Lord that this woman was my mother; I would have had it no other way!

Secondly, I would also like to dedicate this to my father, **Frank P. Mercardante**, who died on June 30, 1974. I am also so thankful for him being my dad and all that he taught me in the short 19 1/2 years he was in my life. I think back on these two parents and know that without them, I would not be doing what I am today and this book would never have been written.

Finally, I want to dedicate this book to my nephew, First Sergeant **Luke J. Mercardante**, who was killed in action on April 15, 2008, while he served as acting Sergeant Major of Combat Logistics Battalion 24, 24th Marine Expeditionary Unit in Afghanistan. He had previously served as an Assistant Marine Officer Instructor in VMI's Naval ROTC from March 2003 to July 2005. His example as a Christian, father, and a Marine was an inspiration for those of us who from time to time have found the journey getting tough. He never gave up!

Table of Contents

Introduction 9

Chapter 1: This Is the Truth!..15

Chapter 2: Comfort One Another 25

Chapter 3: I Need Help! 29

Chapter 4: Mom: From Hate to Love 35

Chapter 5: Inevitable Results 45

Chapter 6: Years of Struggle, and, Oh Yeah, Dad 51

Chapter 7: God, Church, and Intimacy 59

Chapter 8: Setting Down Proper Foundations 67

Chapter 9: Love vs. Agape 73

Chapter 10: Substitutes 95

Chapter 11: The Cycle of Pain.......................................103

Chapter 12: Breaking the Cycle 121

Chapter 13: Verses to Meditate On................................137

Chapter 14: But I've Made Such a Mess of Things!.......149

Chapter 15: Entering His Presence 157

Chapter 16: Going Deeper 167

Conclusion 179

Introduction

After 20 years of being pastors, in January 2005 Rose and I resigned our church. Later that month I left for New Zealand. Rose was not able to join me right away, because she had to finish three more months at her job and also had to train our three sons (who were still at home) how to take care of things while we were away.

I left that day without any real knowledge of what we would be doing when I arrived in Taupo, which is situated in the center of the North Island of New Zealand. To say that Taupo is a beautiful place is without a doubt an understatement. All we knew was that this new chapter of our lives was to be the beginning of perhaps the greatest adventure of our lives. I was going to be a part of Father Heart Ministries, the ministry founded by James and Denise Jordan.

Five years earlier (1999) we had met James and Denise at a conference that we attended in Myrtle Beach, SC. They were the featured speakers at a meeting sponsored by Jack and Trisha Frost and Shiloh

Place Ministries. This was not a chance meeting for Rose and me but rather was one that ultimately would help shape our destinies.

We invited James to visit and preach at our small church in Jefferson, GA, in February 2002, but his schedule would not permit his arrival for some time. After a coincidental cancelation in his schedule, he contacted me around May and we agreed to a September meeting that year. Something about this hunter-turned-preacher captivated us and our church and the thousands of other people around the world to whom both he and his wife over the years have ministered.

Another meeting was scheduled in 2004. This time Jan and Sandra Rijnbeek, who then were ministry assistants, traveled with James and Denise. During one of those times when the six of us were having a "cupper" (that is, a cup of tea), James made an amazing statement. With those eyes that seemed to look right through you, he mentioned how he believed that the pastor at the church where he once had served might need a sabbatical.

Then he said he believed Rose and I needed a sabbatical as well. "Wouldn't it be something if you and Rose could just switch places with that pastor and his wife for about three months?" For one like me—one who was not settled in my spirit as to the place of ministry I should be in—this really hit home.

Lots of things transpired over the next year-and-a-half, but no, I didn't switch places with this other pastor. Rather, through many amazing and not-so-amazing circumstances, I found myself on a New Zealand Air aircraft heading for what to us seemed a little like what we believed the Garden of Eden must have been like!

On that plane, 30-something-thousand feet in the air, I began to go through a real emotional breakdown. I now was on a course for our lives that we both fully agreed was right for us—and that we believed with all our hearts the Father had ordained. I wasn't having what might be considered second thoughts. No, it proved to be much deeper than that and occurred at a time in which I probably would learn the most valuable lesson I would ever learn.

For the past 20 years that I had been a pastor, both Rose and I lived and breathed that role. Of course we experienced good and bad days, but we were immersed in ministry—whatever that means—and to the best of our ability were doing the things that pastors do: preaching, teaching, visiting, counseling, loving people, getting beat up by some of those people, and on and on I could go.

For the better part of 20 years I wrote an article for the local newspaper. A small photo of me accompanied each. I mention this merely to say that I was fairly well known in this community. Whether this was good or bad depended on who you were. Everywhere I went, I was known as *the preacher*, an affectionate term often used here in the South.

If I went to the grocery store, I was *the preacher*. If I filled the car up with gas, I was *the preacher*. Wherever we went and regardless of what we did, I was Pastor Vince Mercardante. Whether one called me *the preacher* or *pastor* didn't really matter. I simply joked with people, "Just don't call me late for lunch!"

So while I was on that plane, it suddenly hit me—and boy did it hit me hard: I had just resigned my church and was basically ending a 20-year season of being a pastor. Now I was headed ALONE to a foreign country to work with a ministry that I loved, but I had no idea what I would be doing. I wonder whether Abraham when he left Ur of the Chaldees experienced some of the same feelings that I did.

For the first time in my life I didn't know who I was. I cried out to God, "I don't know who I am any more! I'm not a pastor any more, I'm going alone to a strange land or, should I say, an unfamiliar country, and I only know a handful of people." Since my role would not be "pastor", so to speak, I believed I had lost my identity.

As I was thinking and grieving about all of this and as I wrestled with the fear and uncertainty of not knowing who I was, the Father gently spoke to me and simply said, "You are my son!" This was for me a transforming word of encouragement, excitement, and peace. I didn't lose my identity after all. For the first time ever, I found it! Now I realized, perhaps for the first time in my life, that I was somebody.

About a year-and-a-half later, while I taught in Seoul, South Korea at a YWAM BEDTS School, the Lord helped me to identify in the simplest of ways just who I was. I was sharing about how so many in the Body of Christ today struggle to know who they are. Many in the Body of Christ have a real identity issue. To me, this was evident by all of the "titles" we put before our names and all the "letters" we put at the end of our names on our business cards.

Jokingly, I told the class that we needed business cards about two-feet long just to hold all of these titles and letters. While I shared this, the Lord spoke to me silently but clearly. So on my ministry business card, instead of any letters I may or may not be able to place at front or back of my name, it simply says "Vince Mercardante Sr. DLB"

It is always fun to watch people's response when they read my card. Right away some will ask what the "DLB" stands for, while others brush over it like they know what it means but are still dying to inquire. No, it is not some new degree that can be earned through years of intense study and passing grades. In fact, it cannot be earned at all. For me, it was my newfound identity and one I would not change for anything in this world or in the world to come.

You see, I am simply "DLB", Daddy's Little Boy! I now have friends all around the world who have adopted this "handle" and have changed their business cards to read the same. Ladies, please don't feel as though you are left out. Rose's card says, "Rose Mercardante DLG." I guess you can figure who she is, can't you?

This book tells the story as I experienced it from the beginning to the present. I am brutally honest in so many ways, because I know that the truth has a habit of setting people free (John 8:32). It is not my intent in any way to disrespect anyone that I may mention throughout this book, but I mention them in hopes that you might be able to relate to something that may set you on a course to come to the only One who can heal, forgive, and deliver us!

*Praise be to the God and Father of our Lord Jesus Christ,
the Father of Compassion and the God of all comfort,
who comforts us in all our troubles, so that we can
comfort those in any trouble with the comfort we ourselves
have received from God (2 Cor. 1:3-4).*

Are you struggling with who you are, why you are here, and how you fit in this big world? Have you spent the best of your time, money, and strength trying to "prove" to people that you are somebody? Perhaps you have been trying to convince yourself as well that you are somebody. This book takes you on my journey, which I have to believe is not too dissimilar from yours.

Come with me; together let's find out who we really are and to whom we really belong. Once we find these things out, I believe it will be the beginning of our enjoying the life and privilege the Father intended for us to have. Knowing who you are, by the way, eliminates most of the questioning as to why you are here!

Chapter 1

This Is the Truth!

S ometimes I think that in our sincere efforts to encourage and bring healing and freedom to people, we inadvertently either misinform them, leave out some important details concerning the realities of life, or at best, overspiritualize the truth. In our zeal to bring people into a realization of the revelation we have discovered, we often paint a picture that sometimes distorts apparent reality. Thus, once our listeners recognize and experience this—realizing they are not experiencing the "good life"— they many feel empty, misinformed, and at times perhaps even disillusioned.

Some even begin to believe they are not good enough to enjoy the freedom we have shared with them or at best feel inferior and not worthy to receive as we have. From this point of view, these dear folks are set on a journey of striving to obtain the things we are teaching and experiencing, which may be truth but which can only be obtained in rest. So, on they go from school to school, conference to conference, and seminar to seminar trying to "get it", whatever "get it" means! The results for many can be discouragement and frustration and even can bring them to the point of giving up.

The great faith teachers fail to tell us that there will be times when we just seem to have no faith. I know that statement, in and of itself, lacks faith, but should we experience these times, they make us feel as though something is terribly wrong with us. The prosperity guys really do encourage and inspire us, but if the time ever arrives when we can't pay the mortgage or when we lose our jobs, we are left feeling as though something is terribly wrong with us or perhaps we are not as good or pleasing before God as "they" are.

In both of these cases, well-meaning but often very harsh brothers and sisters will chastise us because of our "lack of faith" or will rebuke us for what clearly must be some unresolved sin issue lingering in our hearts and lives keeping us from the "fullness" of God's promises. May I suggest to you that at times some of the meanest and most confusing words we might hear are things such as, "You have to . . ." or "You must . . ." or "You'd better . . .".

The evangelist gets us all fired up, but when we knock on that first door and get cussed out or witness to a dozen people with no results, we may go home dejected and never try again. The truth is that times will occur for all of us when we seem to fall short in some areas that we have been taught we should be excelling in. The fact is that these may not be "failures" at all but a part of the process of learning and growing that we must all go through.

Between the years 2000 and 2002 we had nine teams from Brownsville First Assembly Church arrive at the little church Rose and I served in Jefferson, GA. You may remember that from 1995 until around 2005, the Lord moved mightily in and through that church. In many ways the world was impacted by what God was doing there.

Of the nine groups that visited us, only two were invited, but they had fallen so in love with our little church (and we with them) that they just continued to return. We surely were glad they did! These young people would leave the nest of the revival and pour themselves out into our lives, our church, and our community. It was just wonderful!

On one occasion, Rose and I had a chance to go to Brownsville to be with some of our newfound friends and spend a few days. It somehow worked out that we got to sit in on the graduating class of their Bible School that year just as the graduates were discussing the things God had been doing in their lives. This was an absolutely wonderful and inspiring group of about 25 young people who were truly on fire for God. We were really encouraged as we heard story after story of how the Spirit of God was moving in and through the lives of these young people.

It was truly amazing for us to be with these folks as each one shared his or her story. One of the students told us about his recent weekend experience. He had gone by invitation to a town to speak to a group of people that really wanted to be impacted by the revival. They were hoping that through the experiences of this young man and his participation in the revival, something of value would be imparted to them. I am sure this happened!

This same scenario was happening all over the USA; the Spirit of God was really moving through these young people, just like He did at our little church. The meetings were to be held in a building that held around 200 people, but nobody was sure how many would attend.

There was such an overwhelming response to the first meeting that the place was full to capacity, so other meetings were immediately scheduled. I think he said they met around six times and each time "packed the house." I still remember his enthusiasm and zeal along with the genuine cheers and exhilaration from all the students as he spoke.

While he and others spoke, I sensed, however, that there was an unhealthy expectation that was void of reality. You see, these kids went in and out every day, so to speak, from the Mother Ship (Brownsville) receiving and then went out somewhere and poured out what God was doing in them. Week after week for some, they would take what they had received, go unload it at some city or church somewhere, and then quickly hurry back to Home Base, where they felt safe, protected, and secure.

It seemed to me that at least for some of these young people, it was as if Brownsville was the only place where the Spirit was moving powerfully and that it would continue that way forever. Perhaps it should have, but sadly it did not!

Sometimes I have this impulse to bring a perspective that can sometimes be described as being a *spoiler*—being negative or just plain insensitive. OK, Rose says that sometimes I just can't keep my mouth shut. This is something for which I pray for help and deliverance very often. But once again, at this time I just could not keep silent. So, and often much to the fright of my dear wife, I spoke up. Hey, they invited me there, so surely they wanted to hear what I had to say, right? Not!

I told them that I was so excited and thankful for what God was doing in and through their lives. I encouraged them to continue on in the anointing and boldness they were moving in, because the "Church" really needed what they had. But (here it goes) I wanted to know the present spiritual conditions of those 1,200 people that were powerfully impacted by the meetings the young man had had.

I told them that as a pastor, I was concerned for the present well-being of these people and wondered who was taking care of them now that the frenzy seemed to be over. Sure they were blessed out of their socks, but what about now? The deafening silence and the shrugging of the shoulders confirmed my fear and suspicion. And then there came the admonishment they did not want to hear or believe.

I told them that they could not and would not stay there (the Mother Ship) forever. I said that one day they were going to have to leave Brownsville, check into a perhaps dry, unenthusiastic church somewhere, and be a good steward of the deposit God had placed within them. I told them that one day they were going to have to leave, settle down, get a job, rear a family, and "do life"! Well, as you can imagine, once again I was throwing cold water on their fire . . . or so they thought.

I doubt that any of those students in that class that day are still in that church anymore. The school, as it was, closed, the revival fires cooled, and thus the peeps were forced out of the nest to fly for themselves. Over the last several years now we have been able to hear from several of those young people that came to our church. As I had predicted, they have jobs and belong to churches that will perhaps never compare to the excitement of Brownsville. Many have settled down into a job and a marriage. And so, they are now "doing life"!

After things closed in Brownsville and the enthusiasm and fire they were living in waned, many of these kids were just out there somewhere wandering around almost like zombies. Many went into what appeared to be a self-imposed exile as they were forced to face the disillusionment and reality of their "new" lives.

Perhaps some of that happened because of the events that led up to the drastic change in the status of their school, but nonetheless, many young persons left dismayed, discouraged, and disappointed. Without any warning, for some, overnight "life happened". They were forced to sink or swim. I imagine that the sense of loss mixed with fear and no doubt much confusion was very hurtful.

Do we do enough to prepare people for the inevitable "lows" of life? I know it sounds like I have settled for something that is less than God's best. Well, I certainly have not, but I have begun to realize that for whatever reason, most of us do not always walk in what we would call God's best. Should we? Absolutely! Do we? Mostly, no! The fact is that much of what we may think isn't God's best might just be; it is His way of causing us to grow through it.

For most of us there is still that old-time struggle between the flesh and the spirit of man that has been rejuvenated and inhabited by the Spirit of God. Unfortunately, because we are still in this world though not of it, there is a battle going on within us daily. All too often our biggest enemy is ourselves and the problems we cause as we wrestle with ourselves.

From time to time we still seem to get bad news, hear frightening reports about world events, face family and personal problems, and have to deal with people who can often be difficult. (That was gentle, wasn't it?) At night we lay our heads down in an imperfect, sinful world and wake up to the same. For most of us that is the reality of life. And in this environment we need to walk in faith, prosper, and evangelize. Sadly, at times we stumble and falter.

Now I know we are in the world and not of it. I know we are heirs and joint heirs of Jesus Christ. And I know we are Kingdom people and have been given the "keys" and the "authority" to live above the circumstances we so often live through. But again, the sad fact is, while we are gaining the courage to fully trust the Father in every area of life, we often stumble and live lives that certainly do not reflect what most would say is Kingdom living.

I have a dear friend who in the last few years has developed a close and more intimate relationship with the Father. I first met him at a Father's Love seminar; he was so eager to learn and receive. In his zeal to receive but not really feeling the experience he was being taught about, he left a bit discouraged. In his mind he "didn't get enough" and believed he "needed more" teaching.

So, off it was to another school and then another and then another. Three years later things were still much the same. Literally traveling around the world, this dear brother was trying to validate and experience an experience he was taught that he should be experiencing. While he was gaining and learning much valuable information, he was struggling to apply it in his own heart.

When he got home from these seminars and the things he felt while in the seminar didn't seem be there when he settled back in to his "normal-life routine", he would leave again on a quest to get more. When doors didn't seem to open for him to go and share what he was learning, he would go to another seminar or school somewhere to get more. He thought that if he only had more, more would happen. Jesus said, *"I have told you these things, so that in me you may have peace. In this world you will have trouble. But take heart! I have overcome the world"* (John 16:33). The word *trouble* here in the KJV is translated *tribulation*. The word in the Greek means "**. . . pressure, affliction, distress or persecution.**" I submit to you that "when" these things are present in our lives, remembering what we were taught in some seminar somewhere may be the last thing we are thinking of.

My wife and I have had the privilege of traveling to many countries to teach on the Father's Love and have helped share in bringing people to a sense of value and purpose that only His love can give. We have watched as time and time again people are moved, changed, and set free when they begin to see that this love is and has always been for and toward them! This wonderful revelation happened to us in around 1998.

It came at a time when I was at the end of my proverbial rope. At the time I had been a Christian for 20 years and a pastor for about 13 years. I can only describe my life as being miserable. In our small church I was teaching or preaching four or five times a week. That meant that I had to be in the Word of God daily looking for another morsel to hand out to our dear congregation. At the time I didn't realize that I was spending all of my time and energy looking for food for others while I myself was starving to death!

I had reached the place where I was suicidal and wanted to leave my wife and sons to run away somewhere and hide. Where God was concerned, I couldn't see how anyone like Him could really love someone like me, mainly because I didn't love myself. I was overly authoritarian to our congregation and through the disguise of perfectionism hid my own desperate needs. To put things mildly, for the most part I sometimes was not too nice to be around, but few ever verbalized that fact to me personally— few, that is, except my wife from time to time . . . or was it more than that?

At home . . . well, let's just say that the guy with all of the problems was trying to keep four sons in order—"making" them do the "right things" to keep them from having problems. These four precious sons had the unfortunate distinction of actually knowing Dr. Jekyll and Mr. Hyde. The transformation usually happened as soon as we pulled into the parking lot of the church and returned to normal as soon as we pulled out after service.

There was never any doubt that I could or would die for my wife or sons if I had to, but the scars I left on all of them painted a much different picture. Still now, after many years of walking in a closer and more intimate relationship with the Father and after having received much healing myself, I remain broken inside when I remember some of the ways I crushed the spirits and hearts of those I loved the most! Only the hope that they, too, can draw from the Heart of God themselves for healing and well-being gives me the desire to go on.

Let me share parenthetically here for the sake of you who are reading this and can relate all too well to my story. I had to go back to each of my sons one by one and with my prepared list in hand ask them to forgive me for the things I did and the ways I could actually remember that I had hurt them. I really think that is a good and necessary thing to do, but it does not end there.

You see, it is not so much what we say in life that counts, but it is who we are that will really leave a mark. We have been taught all of our lives to say and do "what is right". Well, when the "doing" gets hard and we keep messing up, we simply slip into a pattern of just "saying" what is right. And, we can get really good it. Maybe if I say the right thing enough times, people will not notice that my doing is really different than what I am saying.

I think the thing that has perhaps helped my sons and wife the most over the last few years is not so much what I say, although that is important, but what I do . . . and don't do anymore. This would be true on your job, at your church, or at the grocery store, etc. The people in the world are sick and tired of our actions not backing up our well-learned and often well-meant words. The world is sickened by and turned off by the confusing messages we often send.

The world is not looking for perfection but at least for a humility that springs from a life that truly seeks to live the life that is professed. I think the world is mindful enough to know that there will always be events in life that shake us and throw us a bit off-center from time to time. What they are looking for is someone to help them know what to do or who to go to when those times do occur for them. If it is true, and it is, that we as Christians are a reflection (representation and re-presenter) of God to this world, then what kind of picture are we painting?

I think that perhaps one of the things that Jack and Trisha Frost, the couple that we first heard the message of the Father's Love from and who I attribute to literally saving my life back in 1998, said that really encouraged me was that they had not arrived but were on the same journey that we were. For the first time perhaps in my whole Christian experience I began to really hear in my heart that I did not have to be perfect but only accessible and open to the love the Father wanted to pour in me.

After those early days of seminars and conferences at Shiloh Place Ministries, when I did finally get home and settled back into "doing life", when I experienced days of struggling with feeling loved or usable, Jack's words helped me to know that it would be OK. I knew that what I was experiencing then was just a part of the process that the Father was working in and through me and that no matter what, I would be OK. You will be, too!!!

Chapter 2

Comfort One Another

Praise be the God and Father of our Lord Jesus Christ,
the Father of compassion and the God of all comfort,
who comforts us in all our troubles, so that we can
comfort those in any trouble with the comfort
we ourselves have received from God. For just as the
sufferings of Christ flow over into our lives, so also through
Christ our comfort overflows (2 Cor. 1:3-5).

Throughout this book I am going to be sharing some very personal and intimate details of the lives of both my wife and me. The above words of Paul are the reason I am doing so gladly. When I talk about moms or dads or other personal experiences, it is not at all to bring disrespect to them, nor is it to lift up and exalt anyone, but it is done solely for the purpose of prayerfully bringing to you what was given to us—comfort!

As I look back to where I was spiritually and emotionally just 13 or 14 years ago now, I am amazed at what this wonderful Father of compassion, love, and mercy has done for my wife and me. At the same time, I look forward to what this same amazing Papa will yet do in and through us in the days ahead. It is with great anticipation that I look forward to trusting more in the One who alone can transform me into the vessel He has destined me to be.

If God was and is able to bring a great measure of healing and restoration to me and my life, I am assured that He not only can but will do the same for you. This is what Paul is saying in the verses above. As the God and Father of our Lord Jesus Christ comforts us through our troubles, struggles, and those things we think will simply destroy us, we then, in that comfort, can bring the same to others.

There have been many times as an adult man, father of four, pastor, and might I also add, somewhat macho individual (or so I thought) that I found myself crouched in the corner of our walk-in closet, in the dark, trembling and crying. There were plenty of other times that I would simply break down crying, but not just the trickling down the cheek type of tears. No, I am talking about the gut-wrenching, chest-crushing, head-bursting type of crying and groaning! Do you know the kind?

With a bit of embarrassment and hesitation but going forward in hopes that I can fulfill some of what Paul was talking about above, I share another occasional experience. These were those times when I would be thinking very negatively of someone who had turned on or hurt us in some way or who had done something to cause confusion or division in our church.

Anyone who has been a pastor or leader in the "church" knows what I am talking about. You just cannot be a leader without getting shot by "friendly fire". Of course, at the time, you feel it is anything but friendly fire. Really, I think the wounds of a friend are much worse than someone we either don't know or with whom we have had little contact.

If an enemy were insulting me, I could endure it; if a foe were raising himself against me, I could hide from him. But it is you, a man like myself, my companion, my close friend, with whom I once enjoyed sweet fellowship as we walked with the throng at the house of God (Ps. 55:12-14).

These thoughts would far too often be of the most vile, evil, and corrupt nature. As I look back, the thought that some of these things were in my heart is frightening. I can understand a little how we are reading more and more of the most horrendous acts being committed in the world around us. How is it that some people can do such disgracing, degrading, and demonic things to other people? Simply put, they are just following their hearts!

Now it is one thing for someone who has never known and experienced the forgiveness of their sins, the presence of the Holy Spirit flowing in and through them, or having experienced times of being immersed in the love of a Holy God to experience such thoughts. You might expect these vile thoughts from someone who has never experienced the brush of angel's wings during a worship service or who has never experienced dreams or visions from above.

It might be obvious that those who have never broken bread with the brethren, received or brought forth revelation from the Word of God, or stood in the place of authority that could only have been given by a Holy and Just God would think and feel such horrible things. Right? Well, unfortunately not!

What might be even a bit more sobering is my sincere belief that surely I am not alone. It is one thing for sinners to sin. Sinning is what sinners do best; we can hardly blame them for that. No, the problem is when I, and no doubt many other Christians, think, feel, and sometimes even act on the putrefying rumblings of our heart.

It is with this heart that we often wrestle and because of this heart that we get into so much trouble. And it is this heart that Papa wants to cleanse, soften, and mold into one that represents and reflects His heart. So, as you can see, it would be an understatement to say that I was pretty messed up! But alas, this is the reason for putting these things down on paper. It is to show you from whence He has brought me.

It has been amazing to me as I have watched and experienced the Father placing us right into the middle of other people's lives that have or are experiencing some of the very things He delivered us from. It has been from this platform of brokenness that we have been able to participate with the Father in His healing and restoring of many lives.

> *When they saw the courage of Peter and John*
> *and realized that they were unschooled, ordinary men,*
> *they were astonished and they took note that these men*
> *had been with Jesus* (Acts 4:13).

There is a new level of authority that seems to come when we declare what He has already done in our lives. When we pour out that which was poured in us, it seems to become healing oil for all who will partake. Comfort one another, my dear brother or sister!

Chapter 3

I Need Help!

O K, I can hear some of you who know me well blurting out right about now, "Ya think?" Well, I admit I did and still do. But there was a culmination of events or emotions or just being sick and tired of being sick and tired that happened to me back around 1997. I share some of this in my book *The Offense of Grace* but want to give a more detailed picture here for the sake of comforting those with the comfort I have received.

As a Christian at that point for more than 22 years and a pastor for more than 15 years, I still did not know the love of God. It seems strange to even write this, but it is true. Of course I knew and had memorized John 3:16.

> *"For God so loved the world that he gave*
> *His one and only Son, that whoever believes in him*
> *shall not perish but have eternal life."*

I used all the available Greek concordances I could get my hands on to find the several Greek words that we translate into the word "*love*". I could put together a fairly convincing message on the subject of God's love for us and feel confident when I was done that I had done a good job, but more so, that people walked away knowing they were loved. Or did they really?

There were many times I had heard a sermon from Luke 15 on the "the Prodigal Son" and had taught it myself many times. I loved the part about the sinful, stinking, sorry son "coming to his senses" and returning to his father. The constant gazing into the horizon for his son's return and the father's open embrace and restoration when the son did return gave me hope and joy. But in many ways I was more like the older brother than I thought. He "saw" this love but apparently never experienced or felt it himself!

So here I was, preaching and teaching four or five times a week, reading my Bible (sadly, mostly for another sermon or teaching), and praying, usually out of desperation, yet I only had a head knowledge of this life-changing love. It was in my head but not in my heart. As I said previously I had the head knowledge but not the experiential revelation of this love.

By the way, when I use the big word *revelation,* it need not scare you. It has often become the favorite by word of some of us Christians who want others to think we received something they have not. The truth is that it is simple . . . well sort of. The word *revelation* can be simplified to mean the "drawing back of a curtain". In this case, it is God by His Holy Spirit who draws back the curtain.

When a curtain is drawn back, we see on the other side what was there all the time! In other words, when we finally receive an understanding, a revelation of, the truth about His love, it means some invisible curtain has been drawn back and we can clearly see what was there all along. His immense and indescribable love for us has always been there, but for many reasons we are often unable to see or experience it the way He would like us to. Thus, living in this love becomes difficult.

I had arrived at the point where even though I could quote the verses and preach the sermons, I still did not really know this love personally. It had not become a part of my life to the point where I had the peace (John 16:33) Jesus promised and the sense that I was really approved by God. Many years ago I heard a preacher say that he saw a vision of thousands of Christians walking to and fro in the earth. The problem was they were basically just skin and bones. In other words, they had the skeletal structure, so to speak, of a Christian, but without meat on their bones.

To me, this was a picture of myself and so many other Christians today. We know about the birth, life, sacrifice, death, and resurrection of Christ, have recognized our sins and the consequences of life apart from Him, and have appropriated His gift of eternal life into our lives. In biblical terms, we have been born again (John 3:1-8). But this is the beginning of a journey that does not stop there. Listen to what Jesus said in the following verses.

> *"I am the way and the truth and the life.*
> *No one comes to the Father except through me.*
> *If you really knew me, you would know my Father as well.*
> *From now on you do know him and have seen him"*
> (John 14:6, 7).

Jesus then became the pathway to the intended destination, which was life and intimacy with His Father. Without this knowledge, without having come to the place where we recognize and embrace this amazing love, we are little more that Christians walking around looking like skin and bones. His love is the stuff that puts meat on our spiritual bones and gives us the strength and energy to live the life and to fulfill the destiny He has for each of us.

Not feeling this love in my own life, I set out on a course to earn it, or at least that is what I thought I had to do. I thought that if I prayed more, He would reveal this love. So, I started praying several hours a day and following some simple ideas I learned from reading books by Dr. Yonggie Cho, at the time the pastor of the largest church in the world in Seoul, South Korea. He is a man who himself prayed for many hours every day. For me it became not only easy but a delight.

However, when I wasn't praying, I seemed to slip back into the empty feeling of not being loved. So, I thought that if I read more of the Word every day, perhaps then He would bless me with this love I so desperately needed. But again, although I learned a lot about Scripture, the emptiness persisted. This can be a bit dangerous in that knowledge, without the ability or know-how to apply it, can be frustrating, discouraging, and I believe the cause for many to give up.

Let me say it another way just for emphasis and understanding. I believe that biblical knowledge without being cradled in the love of the Father can produce misguided and even dangerous biblical teaching. If the Word of God becomes seed that grows within us and produces fruit for the world to enjoy, then, without it being fertilized and nurtured with His love, it more often will produce undesirable fruit!

Both my wife and I tried everything we could think of. We fasted more, worked harder, attended church more, and gave more. Yet when the particular burst of excitement we happened to be enjoying at the time faded, we were left alone with the feelings of emptiness, loneliness, and of not really being good enough for Him.

All of these disappointing experiences, in which we seemed to be trying in a sense to buy what we was not for sale and to earn points from a God who was not keeping score, left us desperate. For me, the culmination of this agony was that I was suicidal. I wanted to leave my wife and sons to just run away somewhere and hide. Of course I experienced extreme anger not only against myself but also anger that flowed to everyone around me.

It was then that we came into contact with Jack and Trisha Frost of Shiloh Place ministries, along with their amazing team. We began to have one of those draw-back-the-curtain experiences. Simply put, they taught us about grace. They said that there was nothing we could do to get God to love us any more than He already did. Subsequently, there was nothing we could do to make Him love us less.

As I said, this set us on a journey that has brought us to this point in our lives where we have learned and experienced so much, but it is far from what is yet ahead. That experience with Jack and Trisha literally saved my life and spared my family years of grief! Of course, I know that it was the Spirit of God leading us to someone who could tell us (comfort) what we should have already known. I am so thankful He did and will be forever thankful to these two wonderful people.

Why was it and why is it for so many of us that we cannot see and experience the love of the Father in the way He has always intended we should? Since it is and has always been His desire to reveal His self to us in an experiential way, and since He made that very clear and possible through Christ, the problem then must be ours. Oh, I would love to blame Satan entirely right now, because that would seemingly release me from any responsibility and action in the matter, but I can't.

The problem for me was that there were too many things in front of the window that kept me from the curtain that God desperately wanted to pull back so I could see. There were things like anger, resentment, bitterness, unforgiveness, and ultimately, hatred. Had it not been that God had already provided a way for me to deal with these things I might be able to cry foul here and blame Him, but I couldn't!

I learned that there were things in my foundation that were causing the building to be unstable. I was a living leaning Tower of Pisa. Things that were said and done and experiences I had during those most formable of years of life had shaped who I was. I began to see that in the years from birth up to maybe 6 or 8 that more than 90 percent of who I am today was formed.

These days we are learning more and more that leads us to believe that even in the womb, the foundation has been started for the development of our character, thought process, and how we view life. The good news is that intimacy with God can restore our foundation and bring us to a place of spiritual wholeness. The problem is that this intimacy is impossible apart from the restoration of our foundation and our beginning to walk in spiritual wholeness. Don't give up; you have hope!

In the following two chapters I want to share some things about both my mom and dad. Before I do, I want to make something very clear. Throughout the narrative—and you will hear it again repeated throughout—I **am not** talking here about "bad parents". For both my wife and I, we believe that our parents loved us and would have died for us if they had to. Unfortunately not everyone can say that. We are so thankful that we can.

In an effort to show you how our foundation can become broken, I will be very honest and revealing. Both of my parents are long gone now, but I honor them and their memory. The Father has taken Rose and me on a journey of healing and restoration. I can honestly say that we are so thankful for the parents we had, and if given the choice, would choose them to be our parents!

No, this isn't about "bad parents". It is, however, about the effects of how all of us were reared and how it set the course of our lives. For some of you reading this, hopefully it will change the course of parenting for you when you do eventually have children. Even our view of God was affected by the way we were reared. Your and my view of God today has been very much influenced by the way we were brought up, a point I will talk about later.

Let me also say this at this point. It would be easy to shut me out right now and write me off as a disgruntled, unthankful son who just can't "get over it"! If I had not begun to repeat some of the same mistakes with my own sons that I believe my parents had made with me, I might tend to agree with you. No, we have to get this fixed or else we will pass it from generation to generation, just as much of it has been passed to us.

Chapter 4

Mom: From Hate to Love

I know the title of this chapter reeks of possible disrespect and dishonoring to my mom, but that cannot be further from the truth. I am fully aware of what Scripture in Exodus 20:12 means when it says, ***"Honor your father and your mother, so that you may live long in the land the Lord your God is giving you."*** Paul quotes this same verse in Ephesians 6:2.

The word *honor* used here, if perhaps I can simplify it, means to reverence them both inside (from the heart) and out (in our actions) and to value them. Listen to what Adam Clarke's *Commentary on the Whole Bible* has to say about the passage in Exodus 20:12.

> *"There is a degree of affectionate respect which is owing to parents, that no person else can properly claim. For a considerable time parents stand as it were in the place of God to their children, and therefore rebellion against their lawful commands has been considered as rebellion against God. This precept therefore prohibits, not only all injurious acts, irreverent and unkind*

> *speeches to parents, but enjoins all necessary acts of kindness, filial respect, and obedience. We can scarcely suppose that a man honors his parents who, when they fall weak, blind, or sick, does not exert himself to the uttermost in their support. In such cases God truly requires the children to provide for their parents, as he required the parents to feed, nourish, support, instruct, and defend the children when they were in the lowest state of helpless infancy.*"[1]

No, this is a story of healing and restoration through the Father's Love and how He turned something the enemy meant for evil into something beautiful and for His glory. This is a story that can be identified with by so many of us. It is meant as a means of hope and encouragement for you to know that this great and unshakable love is calling out to you right now!

Being the youngest of three boys can have its advantages and some disadvantages. As I understand the story, my mom really wanted a girl, but after several years of waiting after their second son was born, it was discovered that there was a female problem preventing my mom from conceiving again.

At the same time, my dad, who lost a leg fighting in WW II, was having some health issues. Their doctor recommended that they move out of New York to the better and less-stressful climate in California. So now, a choice had to be made. Do they move to California right then or wait and chance the surgery necessary for my mom to try for that girl? Regardless of the outcome, both parents made a sacrifice to stay and try for another child.

I can imagine that when my mom found out that she was pregnant again, there was such great joy and anticipation. Back in the early '50s, determining the sex of a child before it was born was not really happening, so when she found out she was pregnant, her greatest hope was that a little girl was on the way.

We have learned much in recent years about how things outside of the womb affect an unborn child. Music, emotions, physical matters, and I believe that even spiritual things have an impact on the baby in the womb. I believe that even during this delicate time for a child, foundations are being laid that can affect that child for a lifetime.

So, on September 13, 1954, after nine months of my parents' waiting, hoping, and praying, I entered the world. How does a parent deal with the mixed emotions of joy from the new life that has just arrived and yet the disappointment that it is not exactly what you wanted or expected? I can only relate to this from our own experience when my fourth son was born.

Rose had always wanted a little girl. We just thought it seemed reasonable that after already having three sons, it would be a sure thing. My older brother by this time had had four sons followed by a girl, so maybe this was our chance for a girl as well. When Micah, my fourth son, was just born, my first thought was, "Yeah, another boy!", but, I didn't say a word and waited for the doctor to tell Rose.

When she heard the news, she cried. At first, I thought it was because this boy weighed more than 10 pounds, but when she realized she did not get her little girl, she was heartbroken. She was full of joy and excitement that she had another child, but at the same time she was sad that it was not what she was hoping for. Since that day Rose many times has said that she was so glad she had four boys!

How do children process things in life over which they have no control? Where do they put those fears, frustrations, and feelings that are so often way too big for them to deal with or to understand? Within all of us, deep in our souls, is what we call a "Pain Box". Here each of us begins to store up all of the broken and wounded emotions that travel our way. With each passing day, week, month, and year, our pain box was filling and storing things that would shape our identity!

I remember that one day in the first grade while I attended Catholic School in Long Island, NY, I had done something wrong in class. The teacher warned me a couple of times. Finally, she held up an envelope and said to me that if I did whatever it was I was doing again, she would have me step into the envelope and she was going to mail me to Alaska.

Of course, I did it again and she had me stand in front of the class. With tears flowing down my cheek, I tried to step into the envelope. Now I didn't realize that this was impossible, but I do remember the shame, guilt, and embarrassment I felt at the time. There were many other forms of discipline during this year that caused this little 6-year-old boy to lay many layers in his pain box.

One day this teacher sent a note home to my parents; the note told them about some act of disobedience I had committed. I do not remember the reaction or discipline I received that night, but the next day would leave a lasting impression on me. That day as I sat in the lunchroom filled with kids and ate my lunch, my mom walked in. She walked over to me and proceeded to scream and holler at me and offered some physical punishment as well. I remember feeling shame, guilt, and embarrassment as all of this was taking place in front of a room full of people.

Throughout the years, for whatever reason, my mom was very verbally and physically abusive. For example at times I would struggle with an assignment at school and had to bring the work home to study to bring up my grades. I remember often bringing home the small list of spelling words to memorize. I remember the struggle I often had to get them right. My mom would scream at me and at times hit me if I could not learn these words fast enough.

I don't think we as parents realize how lasting of an impression our words and actions have on our children. To this day I am a terrible speller and am so thankful for the "spell check" feature on the computer. Paul understood the tendency for those parental words to bring pain and in Ephesians 6:4 wrote, ***Fathers, do not exasperate your children, instead, bring them up in the training and instruction of the Lord.***

As I began to grow physically, it didn't take long before the physical hitting with her hands stopped, as it began to hurt her too much. So it seemed that whatever she could find to hit me with became my tormentor. Of course there was the striking with the belt, but I also remember having a wooden hanger broken over my shoulder and one time even a wooden broom. Once in a fit of rage she even broke my guitar over my back. One time she was so angry that she spit in my face, not to mention the verbal, almost sailor-like words she sometimes used towards me.

Both my parents were Italian; I have always enjoyed my Italian heritage. One distinct feature of many Italians is that they have rather large noses. My mom's was not by any means unattractive, but it was an Italian nose. One day, while I sat next to her on the couch, I looked over and noticed her nose. Before I could get the words completely out of my mouth, "Mom, how come you have such a big nose?" her hand shot around and cracked me across the face. At the time I would have been around 8 or 9.

Over the years I experienced many times of expressed verbal and physical anger. I am fully aware that had she done some of these things today, she would have gone to jail or at least had her children taken away from her. This especially would have occurred with the event that took place while I was in the fifth grade.

Mrs. Putnam had sent a note home to inform my parents of my misbehaving in class. Again, I do not have any recollection of what transpired that evening at home, but I very well remember the next day. I was sitting in the back of the room in a double-seated desk alongside another boy when I looked up and saw my mom at the door of the class.

She motioned for me to come to the door, which I immediately did. When I got there, she proceeded to scream at me. She beat and scratched me to the point of drawing blood. The class and teacher, along with me, were in shock. The teacher immediately called for the principal to get her off of me. Needless to say, for my own protection, Mrs. Putnam never sent home any more notes to tell of my misbehavior, even though there were still many times she could have!

That night when I was asleep, my mom entered my room and woke me up. I will never forget what she asked me that night. She said, "Vinny, did I hurt you?" Now just like the other times, that day I felt shame, guilt, and embarrassment. But that day there were two other emotions I remember feeling. I felt anger and hatred toward my mom.

That day I made a decision in my heart. I swore that she would never hurt me again, at least emotionally. I did not realize at the time what I had actually done, but I understand today that I severed the spirit of sonship between my mother and me. Yes, throughout the years, there were other events that happened, but I had built a strong wall in my heart in which to keep her from hurting me emotionally any more! This was when the pain box really started to get filled up.

The last time there was any kind of violence was on the day I told my mom and dad that I was getting married. I was still 17, as was Rose. Our plan was to get married three days after my 18th birthday. When I told my parents, they both erupted in anger. My dad said that the marriage would not last a year.

On the other hand my mom wasn't so nice. She grabbed a hammer and chased me around the house and finally into the garage. Now the whole time this was happening, I was laughing, so you have to get the picture. My dad had lost his leg in WW II and had a wooden prosthesis, which made him walk with somewhat of a limp.

As my mom was chasing me with the hammer, screaming and yelling at me with each step, I had no trouble staying just out of her reach, but my dad was somewhat running and hopping behind her as he tried to grab her and grab the hammer away. It really was both comical and tragic at the same time. He finally caught up with her in the garage, but I could not help chuckle at the whole scene. Of course my chuckling did not help matters at all!

It was from this springboard that I entered into the world of "adulthood" on my own. Both my wife and I began our lives together as we carried the inevitable set of baggage everyone carries in life. As we would soon find out, not only did we enter our marriage with our own baggage, but we started working on our own combined set as well. I can tell you, it makes for a lot of *stuff* to carry around everywhere.

I cannot end this chapter without telling you about the rest of the story. I went through many years of personal and internal struggles dealing with the anger and bitterness I had developed for my mom. One day through a set of circumstances I encountered while I prepared for a book report for a college course I was taking, I finally blew my top.

For three days I was an emotional wreck. Finally, on that third day, I heard the Lord speak to me and say, "If you don't deal with this, your growth with me will stop right now!" Well, I guess that shook me a bit. I calmed down enough to call my mom that night. I had my usual phone conversation with her, which usually consisted of vague pleasantries, but at the end of our conversation before I said goodbye, I told her I loved her.

After what seemed like an eternity of silence, she responded back with the same. I don't know how to explain what happened that day between my mom and me, but something seemed to break between us in our spirits. Subsequent conversations seemed to be more enjoyable; all ended with this new ending, "I love you." Although there was a lot of work I had to do with the Lord and many tears yet ahead, I believe we got to the place in which my mom and I were enjoying our best relationship ever.

I do want to say here that for me, this was a process and not an overnight occurrence. There was something else that was amazing. I never questioned, accused, or confronted my mom on anything she did to me in the past when I was young. But, as I began to forgive her in my heart, it seemed that her heart was becoming more and more open and loving toward me, just as mine was toward her!

During one conversation she said to me that she knew she had treated me badly when I was young. This shocked me, since it had nothing to do with whatever we were discussing at the time. As time went on, the more I would forgive and release, the closer we seemed to become. Now, instead of the usual two- or three-month wait between phone calls, I was calling her at least once every two or three weeks. At the time we lived in different states.

It was in November 2009 while Rose and I attended a conference sponsored by Jack and Trisha Frost of Shiloh Place Ministries that we first met James and Denise Jordan. During one of James' messages he spoke about the healing God years earlier had brought between him and his dad. But even though healing had occurred, apparently James was still a bit distant from his dad.

James said that God spoke to him one day and said, "How can you be a son to me when you can't even be a son to your own dad?" All I can say is that that statement hit me like a ton of bricks. After that session I went back to the hotel room and immediately wrote my mom a three-page letter. In it I spent three pages doing nothing but blessing her.

I asked her to forgive me for things I, as a child, had done that hurt or disappointed both her and my dad and told her that if I had it all to do over again and could choose my parents, I would chose her and my dad. I must say the words literally poured out with little thought onto the pages. When we arrived home a couple of days later, I promptly put the letter in the mail.

My mom was living at the time with my second brother and his wife, as she lived with them and they cared of her. Since at this point she was very sick with emphysema and was having to use oxygen and was unable to move around very well, they would bring her the mail every day. My brother said that when she read my letter that day, she cried and cried and did so for three days. She would die about 30 days later.

My two brothers and I were able to spend several days with my mom at the hospital before she finally died. I can't tell you how blessed I felt that the Father led me to write that letter. It was as if there was finality to the restoration that had taken place between us. I can promise you, it doesn't get any better than that.

My second brother and I were able to officiate at her funeral. To me it was an honor and privilege to have a part in her service. I will forever be thankful to the Father for this gift!

[1] Adam Clarke's *Commentary on the Whole Bible*

Chapter 5

Inevitable Results

As I said earlier, as parents we often do not think about how our actions affect our children later on in their lives. For me, being reared in what I considered as an angry, explosive, and often unpredictable home, things did not turn out too good for me.

By the time I got into high school, I was an angry, unpredictable person myself. Having some size to me by then, I used my anger as a defensive tool to be left alone. I quickly learned that my size along with an angry look and quick temper went a long way as far as intimidating and controlling others. Many people were afraid of me, so that fit well into my desire to just interact with those I wanted to. It all culminated two weeks before graduation.

I had assaulted a student off of campus, but when the school heard about this, it made the decision to expel me from school. The school added to the charge of battery the fact that I had just started working at a bank. Since working full time before being age 18 and working after 11 p.m. was illegal in California at the time, the school had an easy out. With only two weeks left to go, the school believed it was safer to get me out of there. Fortunately, my dad spoke to the principal and at least got my diploma, but I never got to go through the graduation ceremony.

Three months after I was kicked out of high school, the student I assaulted married me. I never saw my dad strike my mom or hardly raise his voice at her, but I had such a jealous rage inside of me that one day, thinking Rose was cheating on me, I beat her. This was not the first time I had been overly aggressive with her; it wouldn't be the last!

Rose and I met when she was in the 10th grade and I was in the 11th. My cousin introduced us; right off the bat, an attraction seemed to occur between us. From the beginning, I was jealous and worried that someone or something would take her away from me.

Turning on the charm, I wrote Rose poems and brief notes assuring her of my love and the fact that life just couldn't go on without her. All of this was sincere and heartfelt, but I wonder how much of it was unknowingly done out of control and my fear of rejection. Don't tell Rose that I said so, but since I was a high-school jock and extremely handsome on top of that, she just couldn't live without me! (LOL)

I really had an unhealthy control on Rose in that my jealousy caused her to draw into herself. When we were in public, she would keep her head down for fear that I would think she was looking at some other guy. I would intimidate her by raising my voice, being quiet, or just ignoring her when she didn't do exactly what I thought she should.

You would think that by her showing me absolute faithfulness and always going out of her way to please me, I would calm down and be at peace in our relationship. But sadly, I did not; many times I know she was just plain afraid of me. I don't think I ever consciously used this "control" to get things, but I controlled nonetheless.

I feel sure that along the way of our courtship, I broke her spirit (although I didn't know then what that meant) and certainly humiliated her many times. Now let me be clear here and say that Rose was no pushover. She was and is extremely intelligent and talented, but for a long time I believe I kept her in such fear and uncertainty that it kept her from obtaining some of the dreams and aspirations she had as a young girl.

During our first year of marriage I still would have times of uncontrolled anger and rage. Drinking didn't help, nor did my constant need for approval and value, which I tried to get from everyone and everything around me. So it was not surprising that no matter how much Rose tried to please and satisfy me, she was unable to quench this deep-rooted empty and wounded spirit within me.

It was during this time that she did something that stirred the rage in me again and I almost killed her. As she lay semi-unconscious on the floor of the bathroom that day, I remember the fear, remorse and shame I felt and the thought that I really needed help. Let me say here and let me make it very, very clear: Rose never did anything that warranted what I was doing to her! Nothing makes it acceptable to beat, abuse, torment, or humiliate another person!

As I picked her up and put her on the bed, I cried out to God for help. I realized that if something didn't change within me, I would one day kill her or someone else. Please understand that I am not blaming my mom or anyone else for my actions here, but I am saying that there are patterns, examples, and foundations laid within us that set the course for our future life.

I have come to realize that our experiences in early childhood form a grid within us by which we view ourselves and the world around us. I liken it to our being given a set of glasses; through those glasses we see and thus respond to everything.

Just think about it. How did we learn what love was except by the example of what was called love and demonstrated to us as a child? Where did we learn how to react when good or bad things happened to us? Who taught us our view of life toward ourselves or others that we might encounter in life? Regardless of the quality of our formal education, an education given to us in those early, most formative years has affected us throughout life.

At one point while I was a teen-ager, I did not want to get married because I was genuinely afraid that I would one day hurt one of my children. So, when Rose and I got married, I swore to myself that I would never do to my kids what I believed was wrong with what my mom did to me. I made a conscious decision that I would be different and would do a much better job of rearing my kids and of showing them real love.

Then in May 1975, we both walked an aisle of a church in La Mesa, CA, and accepted Christ. When we received Christ, there was real and noticeable change in our lives, as there should be. It was amazing to see some of the things that just seemed to disappear out of our lives and the things that now brought a discomforting conviction.

Armed with the Sword of the Spirit and the conviction to live our lives for Christ, we began to have children. In June 1976 our firstborn son, Vince, was born; in July 1979 our second son, Jed, was born. By now we were very involved in our church. We were serving in whatever capacity we could and enjoyed the Word of God and the fellowship of the saints.

We had risen to a place in our church in which people noticed our devotion and service. The pastor loved us. He was a genuine encouragement to me personally and seemed to take me under his wing. It looked like we were on our way to wherever it is you go when you get real spiritual and begin to make a name for yourself.

But there was a dark secret that I assumed was not noticeable to anyone at church or anywhere else. I found myself doing some of the same things to my boys that my mom had done to me. I was verbally abusive and acted more like a drill sergeant than a dad. I would humiliate my sons in front of others—the very thing that had so shamed me.

My second son, Jed, more than any of the other boys really experienced the worst of my behavior. It wasn't until years later that I realized why. Jed looked so much like me. His looks and mannerisms were such a mirror image of me that at times it was a bit scary. I realized just a few years ago that back then, when I looked at Jed, I was seeing me. And since I didn't like who I was, I seemed to take out the hatred I had for myself on him. Although he always was, and still is, a very talented young man, I couldn't seem to give him the love and support that he needed and deserved.

By the time son three (Joshua) and son four (Micah) came along, I was on a course of some healing but still was far from being right. Perhaps some of it was just age and experience, but the last two boys did not get the full wrath of dad as the first two did. But even so, things were said, implications were made, lack of affection was evident, and of course, there was "the look" for them to contend with. Although maybe not as severe, nevertheless, these sons were also very much wounded!

I feel I need to interject this right at this point for those of you who are beginning to recognize that you, too, have some serious issues that are being played out toward your own children. It is one thing for an adult to say that these things were in the past and that we need to "just grow up and get over them." The sad fact is, however, that doing this is nearly impossible without help!

But here is what I want you to consider. You may be saying or thinking that you can and will just grin and bear it; you may just do that. But, consider the children. Do you realize that you are laying a foundation of hurt and insecurities in them that may cause years of pain and problems for them? Like you, they will one day feel at the end of their ropes and in turn pass along on to their children the same pain that you passed on to them.

What I am saying, dear one, is to please get help. Allow the Father to bring comfort and healing into your heart right now and to restore the broken areas of your heart. The healing you receive now will not only pay tremendous dividends in your own life but can and will bring a new inheritance to your family perhaps for generations to come.

Chapter 6

Years of Struggle, and, Oh Yeah, Dad

I remember the shock I felt one day in the late '90s when I realized that the church at which Rose and I had served as pastors, at that point, for about seven years was the longest I had ever been in any one position my whole life. I was at the previous church for two weeks short of five years, which made that the second-longest run in my whole working career.

It is not that I didn't like to work; the problem was that I didn't like people to tell me what to do, especially if they did so in angry, offensive, or arrogant ways. In fact my very first "real" job as an adult was at a bank working in its computer center in San Diego, CA. This was the job that I got just two weeks before high-school graduation.

I got along well enough with my boss at the time, but he left suddenly. Management decided to take me and another man who was in an equal position to me, just under the shift supervisor, and give us each a turn running the shift. The problem was that this other guy was, in my opinion, arrogant, and cocky; what's worse, he got to have the first turn at being in charge. I called in sick the first two nights. On the third I called in and said I was not coming back!

That proved to be the beginning of a lot of years of just wandering from job to job. Along with all of this was the required moving from place to place. In the first seven years of our marriage we moved five times—not always because of a job, but still, it was a bit much. As, I look back, it is a wonder that Rose held on, especially when the fifth move was to another state.

During this time, while I did not realize it, I was looking for a father figure to enter my life and, well, father me. My dad died when I was 19; to me he was a great father, but there was not a lot of intimacy between the two of us nor, I suppose, between him and my brothers. The need for a father figure and the need for intimacy were things I pursued without realizing what was I was doing.

Dad just couldn't do it! Now I know that seems strange to say, but it is with the greatest respect for his memory that I say it. I had a great love for my dad. In fact it took me nine years to grieve his death. My dad just didn't know how to be intimate with his sons, nor did he know how to nurture us the way we needed. The same could be said about my wife's dad, who, while loving his family deeply, just could not show it in ways most important to a child.

I want to share a little about both of our fathers just to give you some understanding of what I mean. Please know that it is with the greatest respect and honor for these two men that I share. My hope is that in sharing their story from our perspective, you perhaps can relate to your own life or that of your dad. While Rose and I may have known these things about these men for years, it was not until the late '90s after 25 years of marriage and lots of heartache that we began to understand our roots.

My dad was born in 1919 and reared in the Bronx in New York. Being one of eight siblings, two of which died very early, and like in any family, I am sure he had to make his mark, so to speak, in the family. His father was in the ice business delivering ice door-to-door for people's iceboxes. Obviously, this was before the refrigerator became popular.

I am not sure exactly when, but my grandfather became ill and eventually died, leaving his wife to rear and care for six kids. As bad as losing a dad is for any child, I guess it was particularly tough on my dad because his father died on the day my dad turned 12! No doubt the kids knew their father was sick, but when the inevitable happened, it would have had a devastating effect. Now, my dear grandmother was left with the grieving of the loss of her husband and the responsibility of rearing all of these kids.

Now imagine for a moment if you can how this all affected my dad. First, my dad was one of six children and likely had to compete for whatever intimacy and affection his dad had to offer. I don't know how intimate my grandfather was with his kids, but I do know he left his family in Italy at a young age to take a boat to America. Trying to make his way and fortune here in America, my grandfather worked his own business at a time when his business was being taken over by technology. So, besides being challenged to effectively give his kids the love and attention they needed, now he no doubt was emotionally broken as he watched his future crumble.

On top of all of this, when their father died, my father and his siblings were left completely without the financial and emotional support they needed. At age 12 my dad, along with some of his brothers, had to go to work in a grocery store to help support their mom and the other children. As we might imagine, life at that age—growing up too quickly out of necessity—simply added to his dilemma.

Then he "grew up", married my mom, whom he knew since he was a child, entered the United States Army, and fought in WW II. During that time he lost his leg while he fought in France, returned home, and tried the best he could to make do for his family. My older two brothers were born fairly quickly; then I arrived seven years later.

So here we were with a good dad trying to rear his three sons without the personal knowledge or experience of a father having reared him. My dad was always a good provider, but he did lack in the intimacy department. Besides that, with his wooden prosthesis, he was not able to play ball with us or do some of the other things dads often love to do with their kids.

He was very supportive of me and clearly loved me. I always felt that in some respects, whether it was because of his maturing or my just being the youngest, that maybe I was his favorite. I came to realize and fully understand once I started to have my own children, that no parent should have a favorite! But I really knew that he was proud of me when I played sports in school and always attended my football games.

On my wedding day, well, let's just say, he was tolerant. Rose and I both were under 18 when we decided to get married. Feeling that we were way too young, both sets of parents were against it, but knowing we were determined, they relented. My dad and Rose's mom actually had to go with us before a judge and sign for us to get permission to get married at that age. They went with us because my mom and her dad refused.

So, here comes the big day. The entire day before my wedding, my best man and his parents begged me to reconsider and even offered me a "way out". Knowing that Rose just couldn't live without me (lol), my friend and I left for the church. In one last plea just before we pulled into the parking lot of the church, he said "Merc, let's get out of here!" I told him OK; we turned around and left.

But, a couple of miles down the road I made him turn back. When we did arrive at the church, needless to say a little late, I was met by my dad, my two brothers, and her dad. None of them looked too pleased, as not only were they not sure about what I was doing, but Rose was waiting at the back of the church, with music playing and a church full of guests.

I will leave it up to your imagination as to what they might have said to me that day. I went in, gladly got married, and off to the reception the happy couple went. I can tell you that in the wedding pictures with Rose and me and our parents, two of the three men in that picture had phony smiles; it showed! I guess the thing that I remember the most now after all these years was the handshake my dad gave me that day. You see, hugging and verbal words of love and affirmation, even on a good day, were just not the norm.

There is no way I could ever blame my dad for his lack of intimacy, since he could not give what he did not receive or know himself was available. Yet the effects of what he did not give us really helped to shape and form the lives of his three sons. Both of my brothers and I tried to be more intimate and affectionate toward our own children. While I think I was successful in that area to some degree, it was clearly not enough!

Rose's dad showed another example of a good man who just didn't have to give what his two sons and three daughters needed. Being born to farmers of German decent, he was the youngest of three siblings. His mother died shortly after he was born; when Rose's dad was about 3, his dad just couldn't work the farm and take care of three children.

One day, his dad took him to an orphanage to leave him "for a couple of months" while he worked things out. He seemed to be able to take care of the other two children because they were a bit older and could help with chores around the house and farm. Those three months passed by; his dad never returned for him.

At 16, Rose's dad lied about his age and joined the U.S. Navy, which became his career. When he got married to my mother-in-law, like any good Catholic family they began to have children quickly and ended up with five. Working very diligently in the Navy, my father-in-law progressed up the ranks about as far as he could for an enlisted man.

He was in charge of several hundred men and was able to manage them well. The only problem was that without the foundation of a father's love as a child, he didn't know how to father his own children. Since he was successful in the Navy and could easily order his people around, he used the only tactic he knew and ordered his kids around, too.

Rose said that he was more like a military officer barking orders to his men rather than a dad speaking to his children. Oh, he was a wonderful provider, but intimacy was just something he did not have. He tried to get Rose, his middle child, to learn to bowl, shoot a gun, and golf, all of which she really tried very hard to do to please him. Seeing she just couldn't get it, however, he stopped trying.

It is bad enough for any child when the child believes he or she just cannot please parents. It is worse when a parent lets the child know by both words and actions that the youngster has not and apparently cannot please. That child will often spend his or her life striving to please and to gain the approval of anyone who will give it. Sadly, this can take the child to places and doing things he or she normally never do.

So as you can see, both Rose and I had good, loving fathers, but being in a sense orphans themselves, they were unable to emotionally father their children in the ways a child needs. Their lack of foundation became our lack of foundation; the cycle continued to our children. Unless this cycle is broken, generation after generation will be affected by living from wound to wound. Sadly, along the way, many do not make it.

For me, the sense that I was never good enough, not valued, and not knowing the difference if and when I was, became a big problem. So, even when I did have a good and caring boss, friend, or pastor, I just could not receive it because I didn't know the difference. Perhaps at times I felt the warmth and acceptance emerging from people, but because I didn't know how to respond to it, I simply ran from what I so desperately needed.

Before I end this chapter, I want to share an example of how children can react in life when they feel they just cannot please mom or dad. As I said, there is a tremendous need for children to feel they are valued by their parents and that regardless of their shortcomings, somehow they "fit" in the family. The feelings of not being approved or valued can be either real or perceived.

Several years ago a doctor in our area approached Rose and me for some help. Years earlier he had temporarily lost his medical license because of an addiction to prescription drugs. He had apparently succeeded in passing the probationary period set for him. With the drug-addiction problem seemingly behind him, his license was restored; he was again practicing medicine.

When we met him, he was preparing himself for an imminent divorce and was on the verge of abusing prescription drugs again. In a word, he was at the end of his rope. Not only that, but because of the desperate situation he felt he was in, and overwhelmed with discouragement, he was, I believe, in a place where he was contemplating suicide as the only way out of his pain.

This man had a beautiful wife, herself a doctor, two wonderful children whom he loved and cherished, and a thriving practice. He was extremely educated, having two master's degrees besides his medical degree. On top of that he was very wealthy. He had managed to invest wisely and owned a lot of commercial and residential properties, which all were rented or leased. So, for a guy who seemed to have the world by the tail so to speak, what went wrong?

As we talked through his life and began to do some ministry, we found that this great man was just a broken little boy. He was one of several children—all of them grew up to be very successful in their respective careers. But the one thing our friend was unable to do, regardless of what he accomplished in life, was to please his mother. In his own words he told us, "Nothing I do is good enough for her!"

When he was in college getting those master's degrees, she insisted he could do better. After he became a doctor, it still wasn't enough for her to offer her approval. As he began to accumulate wealth, it wasn't enough. Even his choice of a wife just didn't quite fit into her (mom's) expectations. So, as it turned out, everything this man did in life was to get something from his mom that she was either unwilling or unable to give.

The result of course was a desperate, dejected little boy walking through life with his head down, shoulders hunched, and feeling like everyone in the world hated him. The more he began to feel and then live this way, the more he believed it. Without knowing it he set himself on a course of self-destruction.

Thankfully, he was able to release some of that pain he had stored up all those years and begin to find a place of rest, peace, and acceptance. We sat in for his parents and spoke words of affirmation and love over him. At first, he experienced an incredible outburst of emotion, as years of pain and hurt spilled out. But, after simply speaking words of love over him and expressing a love that he never felt in his life, he ended up like a little boy being held by his mom and dad.

Never underestimate the need and importance of value and acceptance in someone's life. With it, a child can overcome any handicap and thrive under what would appear to be the worst of circumstances. Without it, regardless of the "things" life has to offer and the treasures gained, that person will remain unhappy, frustrated, and empty!

I want to encourage you to tell someone today how special he or she is. There are no doubt people you know right now that are very different than you. They do things you don't do, go places you don't go, and live a life very contrary to the one you live. Yet, they are still just as loved by the Father as you and I are. Maybe, if someone would just see past the veneer of sin they might be involved in and acknowledge their value as human beings, maybe, just maybe, the walls will come down and their hearts will open to the love of our Holy and Just God!

Chapter 7

God, Church, and Intimacy

Rose and I were reared in good Catholic homes and as such, attended church almost weekly. Through the first grade I went to Catholic school, but after we moved to California, the remainder of my education was in public schools. On the other hand Rose completed her first eight years in Catholic schools and has the red knuckles to prove it! (If you have never been to Catholic school, especially 20 or 30 years ago, you will not understand that last remark. If you have, you likely have those red knuckles as well! LOL)

For whatever reason—and not blaming anyone—for us, there was just not much there at the Catholic Church at the time. So, even though we were reared in good Catholic homes, as soon as we got married, we stopped going to church.

About a year and a half after we married, my dad died. The shock and grief of that seemed to thrust us back into going to church. I still remember his priest saying that he saw my dad all the time at church, but for some reason, the priest specifically remembers my dad receiving Communion on the day Dad died.

Anyway, we jumped right in with both feet and immediately became fully engrossed in church life . . . well . . . all for about six or seven weeks. Whether it was because of our remembering why we stopped going in the first place or because we started going for the wrong reasons, our adventure was short-lived. Either way, as adults (or so we thought), it was our decision; we can blame no one for our actions.

Well, as the next year and a half progressed, I became increasingly unhappy with my job and really, with life in general. So, as I mentioned earlier, I quit my job for no good reason at all. With no backup plan, as I struggled for value and approval, I entered into a business deal that was going to make me rich. Perhaps you have heard of such opportunities or tried a few yourself.

During that time, after we gave all the money we could borrow to two guys who turned out to be crooks, we found Christ. One of the two partners who scammed us said he was a Christian and went to church every Sunday. He told us about Jesus and the miracles He did not only in the past but was still doing.

After all the build-up, I agreed that the next Sunday we would go to church with him and his wife. Rose reluctantly agreed but was very hesitant, especially after our Catholic indoctrination that really frowned on attending "other" churches. But at this point in our lives, since we were fairly desperate and hungry for something, we went.

I don't know what Pastor Greg preached on that Sunday, but I do remember that when he gave an altar call to receive Jesus as our Lord and Savior, we both got up and went to the front and received Him. From that point forward, even though life still had its struggles, we could see in ourselves real change, as should be the case.

As a young boy I often had some real strange dreams, many of which were reoccurring. Most, especially the ones that involved God, were filled with great fear. So when we began to understand how loving and kind Jesus was, things went well for us. The Father, on the other hand, was a bit of a different story. With Him I had, at best, some fear and reservations.

My view of God was that He was a Giant Police Officer in the sky with a lightning bolt in one hand and a vial of deadly disease in the other and that He was just waiting for me to make a mistake so He could throw one or the other at me to punish me. Over the last 36 years of our walking with the Lord, I find that this or similar views are not uncommon among other people.

We learned that we all view God through the mirror image of our earthly parents. They were the ones given the task of projecting to us an image of God the Father—His love, compassion, grace, and mercy, so that ideally one day, the transition to our receiving Him would be a no-brainer. I mean, the thought would be that if God is like this and is apparently much better, why wouldn't I give my life to Him?

Sadly, in my view, even the best of parents fall short of reflecting an accurate portrayal of His love. Perhaps it is impossible, though I have seen many parents who have come close. Unfortunately, I was not one of them. Now, years later, I can understand the reasons behind my view of God, especially in light of some of the things I experienced in those early years. I wonder how my sons today view God.

In the next chapter I will talk in more detail about our view of God and how during our early years it can be determined or at least distorted.

This being the case, I was always on guard at church. Soon after I accepted Christ, I met some folks that attended a fairly new church in town. In their view, the pastor was amazing. We tried going there and quickly found it to be a place in which we seemed to fit in. I felt an immediate connection to the pastor and realized that in him I was seeing the father figure that I really needed, especially now that my dad was gone.

Rose and I became very involved in this church in Lakeside, CA, and seemed to be on our way to "big things", whatever that meant. The pastor and his wife loved us and on occasion even invited us to their home; to us this was both an honor and privilege. I remember how at the beginning of church services, the young men would rush to be the first to meet the pastor so they could carry his Bible to the front.

During this time I started to notice that on the job I worked, I was developing an unhealthy attraction to one of the women on the shift. Never having experienced something such as this before as a married man, and being a young Christian and knowing it was not right, it really scared me. I didn't know what to do. So, the first person I told was Rose so she could pray with me through this. I figured, since I brought this attraction into the light and especially with my wife informed, my forthrightness would be a defeating blow to Satan.

As you could imagine, this was a shock and hurt Rose very much. But fortunately, after Rose realized that I was being very open and was approaching her for help, she wholeheartedly joined in with me. The issue was stopped before it could get started. Praise God! I still believe that enlisting your spouse to help you fight personal attacks of the enemy is a good policy.

I don't know if it was for further help or just because I felt like a little kid around my pastor and wanted to confide in him as I would a dad, I went to see him to tell him what was going on. This happened around 34 years ago, but not until three years ago did I realize how deeply this experience really affected me.

I realized how his reaction that day to my situation further engrained in me and confirmed my feelings about how God was! I didn't understand it back then, but I now see that a pastor really plays a tremendous role in reflecting and representing God to the congregation. To many people in their congregations pastors truly become father figures.

I scheduled the appointment with my pastor/dad (I believe he and his wife also had the same parental feelings about me). As I sat across his desk, with some fear and apprehension I told him about the attraction and my fears and that I had already enlisted Rose's support for help.

His response pierced me then; even now as I think of the response, I am grieved to think that this is how most pastors even today would respond to someone crying out for help. He leaned over the desk, straightened the cuffs on his shirt, and with the most serious, eye-piercing look said to me, **"Vinny (as he always affectionately use to call me), I will not have any fornicators on my team!"**

He did not acknowledge the fact that I had approached him for help before any problems occurred or that I had been open and honest with my wife. What I think I needed at that moment, and something I have done countless times as a pastor myself while in similar situations, was for him to embrace me, to tell me that he would stand with me, and to pledge that we would fight this thing together.

Instead, I got the "look" and frankly, a stern chewing out. Of course, at the time I felt like a dung heap, but I also remember thinking and believing that I had totally messed up this relationship with this father figure and that things never would be the same. Back then, the thought of having lost another relationship such as this was the greatest fear I had.

I don't think my pastor really treated me much differently after that, but I never looked at him in the same way. Oh yes, I still saw the father figure in him, but from that point on I felt I had failed him and had become a second-rate son. This further convinced me of my being a failure and being unable to have any real or genuine intimate relationships, especially with church leaders!

From that point on I found myself going out of my way to do things to earn and warrant the love and affection of the pastors and church leaders I have had over the years. Even when I became a pastor myself, I found myself saying and doing things for people on my team simply to guarantee their friendship and loyalty and to feel a sense of value coming from them.

Because of my insecurities many times I would compromise my own convictions just to feel like I had a measure of intimacy with some people. By intimacy here I am talking about my having the sense of closeness and fellowship that only intimate friends usually have. My compromising was that I often overlooked things that a pastor should probably address in people just to be sure they remained my friends. This certainly is no way to help those the Father has entrusted in our care.

To the many people over the years that I just would not or could not correct, admonish, instruct or even encourage at times for fear of saying or doing the wrong thing that might cause "me" to lose what "I" needed, I ask your forgiveness. I realize that in an unintentional yet warped way, I was using you to satisfy a need in me. I now know that this was conditional love, or as the late Jack Frost used to say, "Love with a hook!"

In truth, when our needs for identity, value, approval, or security take us on a horizontal journey to find the fulfillment and satisfaction we think we need, not only will we fail, but in a way, I believe it is idolatry. Simply put, idolatry is putting something or someone above or in the place of God. When we search for our inner needs to be met by anyone or anything other than the only One who can really satisfy those needs, I believe we sin.

Addictions are, in my opinion, simply our unknowing attempts to medicate (deaden) the hurt and pain we are experiencing inside. While we often put drug addicts and alcoholics way up there on our list of "terrible people", I assure you it is only a list of our choosing. Addictions are not limited to things that make us stumble, slur our words, or take celestial journeys.

For me, stress, fears, insecurities, and doubts usually lead me to the refrigerator. While I certainly know better and by now can just about predict what's next when these feelings arise, it is still an addiction. It is masking a greater problem—the basic need for intimacy and value—and replacing it with something that in this case makes a "big" difference in my life. (Pardon the pun.) I will talk more about this later.

Chapter 8

Setting Down
Proper Foundations

Depending on what you might be reading, psychologists tell us that by the time we reach the age of anywhere between 4- to 6- or 7-years old, as much as 85 to 90 percent of who we become in adulthood has been established. That is, those early years have formed a foundation within us in which everything we think or process is filtered.

You might say that as very young children we begin to see life through a set of invisible glasses that have been form-fitted and adjusted for us by those closest to us at the time. For most of us, those closest to us are our parents. From these experiences in our earlier years we develop a foundation from which most of how we see life and what we do in response to life, as well as how we relate to others and even to our own selves, is established.

When I am teaching about the Father's Love and our understanding and experiencing this love, I like to say it this way: We view God through the mirror-image of our earthly parents. Perhaps I can say it another way: We view all of life and we respond to that life from the perspective and foundation that our early years gave us. I can also make a similar observation to the spiritual aspect of our lives.

Take, for example, your first few years as a Christian. If, when you first accepted Christ into your life, you were part of a church that taught and encouraged Bible reading, intimacy with God, and evangelism, you likely would be someone who for the most part still does these things years later. They thus would have become a part of your foundation.

If you were taught to pray and to seek the voice of God in every situation of life, then you likely still do that now as a mature Christian. Although you may not always seek to hear a word from the Lord, you will likely still feel that inner tug of conscience when decisions need to be made.

I believe the lives of the pastor, elders, deacons, and Sunday-school teachers are extremely important in the early childhood development of baby Christians. The devotion, or lack thereof, that we see and observe in these church leaders will play a major role in our own spiritual development. You can imagine then how the often-occurring moral and ethical failure we see in the church in its leaders is affecting the *"little ones"*! (Mt. 18:6).

Yes, we are responsible to ***show ourselves approved unto God*** (2 Tim. 2:15); we will answer for ourselves (2 Cor. 5:15), but let me say it again: what we observed in those early years has had a profound effect on how we relate to God and life today! It also affects how we see ourselves.

What was your foundation like in the early years of your life? Were Mom and Dad around a lot, or were you a latchkey child? Did mom or dad drink a little too much? Were you often held in a tender way, or were you always kept at a safe distance? Did you hear words of encouragement and affirmation, or were the words you heard often filled with negativity and condemnation? Perhaps you lost a parent, either emotionally or physically, in your early years.

These and many other things that you and I did or did not experience during those very formative years have, for the most part, made us who we are today. Not only that, but when I look into a mirror or relate to someone at work, I do so through the screening process developed in those years. My response to my boss or to the police officer that pulls me over for a traffic violation depends in part on how, in those early years, I learned to relate to authority.

The fact that the family has been severely fragmented in recent decades and that parents have been so preoccupied with work and other things of life is reflected, I believe, in the increasing disregard and disdain for authority. The lack of respect people have today for the police, the elderly, their neighbors, their pastors, and even their bosses is a good indication that the foundational years of so many people has been flawed and fragmented.

Can you begin to see just from what little I have shared so far how important it is for parents to spend quality time with and impart proper affections to their children? Likewise, can you perhaps begin to understand more and more of the enemy's tactics in putting barriers between children and their parents?

I am going to quote the last two verses from the Book of Malachi, which is the last book in our Old Testament. It is fairly well agreed on that after these words, we entered into what has often been called "the silent years". That is, there is a 400-year gap between the last recorded writings canonized in the Old Testament and the writings describing the coming of John the Baptist and then Christ in the New Testament.

Apparently, if there was any, none of the writing that may have been written during these 400 years of "silence" was deemed worthy enough by the early church fathers who were assigned, with the task of compiling the writings, to enter what most of us now know as the New Testament. So, much would have gone on that we can only perhaps find glimpses of through some historical writings. Regardless, I don't think those years are important for us here in this discussion.

Before I quote these two verses, I am going to pre-warn you that what I share about them is likely not what you would find in many commentaries on this subject. It is not that I believe I have anything over those brilliant writers but simply that I want to speak of one of the effects that I see that happened after Christ came to the earth.

I agree with most that "Elijah" mentioned here is a reference to John the Baptist (Luke 1:17, Mt. 11:12-15). But let me assure you that I am not at all trying to present to you a theological thesis worthy of any prolonged debate. I am simply sharing what I see as one of the unquestionable results of Jesus' coming into the world.

> *"See, I will send you the prophet Elijah before that great*
> *and dreadful day of the Lord comes. He will turn the*
> *hearts of the fathers to their children, and the hearts of the*
> *children to their fathers; or else I will come and*
> *strike the land with a curse"* (Mal. 4:5-6).

One thing that is clear to all of us is that family is vitally important, but the family has also suffered many setbacks in recent years. Although there would have been times throughout history, I suppose, that many families seemed to have a "Leave it to Beaver" type of family, I think, however, that the problem of broken families went much further back than we can imagine.

When Adam and Eve were thrust out of the Garden, it would have been a very sad day for both man and God. But it was at that moment, I believe, that the relationship between a man and his wife and parents and their children would have begun a downward spiral leading to where we are today. Call it whatever you like; at that moment, as man entered into a whole different relationship with Father God, the family was in trouble. If man is not daily walking and fellowshiping in the cool of the day with the Father, life can only become an out-of-the-Garden experience!

So to me, when Christ came to restore fellowship between God and man, it set the course for families to be restored as well. And I think for the most part it would almost have to start within families. Why? Because we view God through the mirror-image of our earthly parents. If the image at home is bad, then the image of God most likely will be distorted.

The promise of restoring fathers to their children and children to their fathers is huge. And if the results implied in the verses above is that unless they are restored, the land would be under a curse, it makes it even more understandable. If you would just see the word *curse* here as the absence of blessings, you can understand what we see and live in today.

Broken people equal broken homes equal broken societies and ultimately broken relationships with God. So I feel that a big part of what was accomplished at Calvary was a way for homes to be restored and for people, being able to see clearly now, to then enter into unhindered intimacy with the Father.

I want to share with you in the next chapter what I believe is the establishing of a proper foundation in the lives of our children. I must be honest and say here that this information does not come from the experiences of one who has proven himself by his great example. No, but for the grace of God I would have totally destroyed my boys from any hope of normalcy.

These lessons I have learned came from my trying to walk daily with my heavenly Daddy who has begun teaching me the reasons for my own frustrated journey and from this has placed me on a path of healing which in turn has hopefully helped put my wife and sons on a similar path. After that, everything else is a bonus!

Chapter 9

Love vs. Agape

The New Testament uses the word *love* many times. Depending on which version of the Bible you use, you might notice that the word appears in as few as 157 to as many as 203 verses. The actual number or times the word *love* is used in those verses can range from as few as 180 to as many as 253 times. Anyway, the concept of love is clearly important even if it is based solely on the frequency of its use in the New Testament.

One disadvantage that I think we may have today is in the defining of the word *love* in the English language. I think there is a great deal of misunderstanding as to what love really is. Let me give you some examples of what I mean. If I say that I love my wife, it would have a different meaning than if I say I love my Christian brothers and sisters. Certainly love is demonstrated differently depending on the object loved.

At least in their application, the meaning or at least the expression of both of these would be different from what I would mean if I said

I loved sports. This, again, is why I think we have such an innate and inner need to know and understand what real love is.

I have a dog whose name is Dodge. Dodge loves to jump and stand on his back legs while he reaches up to lick me after I have been gone for a while. In the evenings if my wife and I sit around and watch some television, Dodge will often lay there next to me on the couch with his head on my lap. Sometimes he will stand or sit on my leg and lay his head on my chest. This is his way of saying that he requires some affirmation from me.

In a word, I love Dodge! And, by the way, he loves me. But the love I have for Dodge is far different than the love I have for my boys. You see, love takes on a different shape, meaning, and expression depending on whom or to what we may be ascribing it to. In all of the examples I have used, I believe it would be safe to say that love is an "action word".

There is one thing I really like to say to every young girl that I can. When that boy at school gazes into your eyes with that puppy-dog look and his body language shows signs of total submission and a little tear forms in the corner of his eyes and you can see his heart beating through his shirt and in a soft tender voice he utters, "I love you", you can be sure of one thing: It's a lie!

Oh, he may mean that he "loves you", but he really doesn't "love" you in the sense that both he and you may think or hope he does. Are you confused yet? You see, his love for you is most likely at that moment filled with conditions and manipulation. Love that tells you that it loves you "if" is no love at all! How can we really give or receive love God's way when we do not yet understand it ourselves?

I truly believe that if we are ever to experience God's love in our lives in the way that I think He desires or to be able to express this love to people around us, we need to have some understanding of what real love is all about. Again, I am convinced that few people have really tapped into the understanding of this priceless, eternal love!

Love finds its expression in many different ways, some of which, if we don't really understand, can be a bit confusing or at best leave us questioning motives. Let me share here just two quick examples of what I mean. One is a recent example and the other an ancient one.

Recently, a friend of ours had a dog that for 17 years she loved and cared for. I think that made the dog around 120 in doggie years. Anyway, as age does, the dog began to slow down and develop some physical problems and by this time was in some discomfort and pain. Finally one morning our friend woke to find the dog lying in the middle of the floor and being unable to get up.

Seeing this animal/family member in this condition and realizing that things were not going to get any better, our friend had to make a painful decision. So she bought the dog her favorite treats and spent the whole day with the dog around the fire and even napping with the dog on her doggie bed—just loving and reminiscing with her. Anyone who has ever had a loving family pet can probably relate to what was happening here.

Finally, somehow gathering the strength and will power, our friend took the dog to the veterinarian and had her put to sleep. There is no need to even try to describe the unabashed emotions our friend went through in this whole ordeal. My point is this: What she did for that animal was done out of 100-percent pure love!

Many years ago, before time as we know it began, our amazing God also made a decision because of love. It was not His first, nor would it be His last decision based on love. The decision God made way back in eternity somewhere was made even though He knew it would cost Him personally so deeply.

Knowing that sinfulness would one day grip the yet-to-be-created human race, making it impossible for people to enter into the intimate, loving relationship He so desired for them and with them, He made a heart-wrenching decision. Again, you can be sure He counted the cost very carefully, but love overtook the risks.

So the purest of love began to demonstrate itself. The decision was made to send His only begotten Son to the earth to pay an amazing price to make it possible for man to know His love. The Son would one day take the full weight of every sin—past, present, and future, on His own shoulders and finally would die a horrible death because of it.

Why? It was because of the Father's tremendous heart of love. How? He did it with the full measure of His love. Intimacy with the Father is available to all who will receive the gift, which is His love! God's greatest expression of love was manifested to us through the life and death of His Son, Jesus!

To help understand even a little bit of the price that this love paid, imagine what it would be like if we were called upon to give the life of our own child to ransom a people that usually were unloving, unthankful, and certainly unappreciative. You and I just could not do it. The cost would be too great!

AGAPE

What is a*gape*? Many of us have heard this word used in a sermon or Sunday-school class before and have perhaps heard or used the definition, "it is that God-type of love." OK, *agape* is God's type of love, but what in the world does that mean and what does that look like, and most of all, how does it work? It's amazing to imagine that such a small word can have such a big meaning, but it does. Well, some time back I believe the Lord gave me some understanding of His love and how it worked.

I want to share with you, albeit very briefly and certainly not in any way meant to be exhaustive or all-inclusive, some thoughts on what *agape* might be. Understand that this is a word, concept, and experience that might take an eternity to completely unfold and understand. Then again, we will probably understand it completely immediately on our entrance into the Father's presence!

For the sake of this discussion I am going to refer to the heart as that which is inside of us—the center of our being that gives us the ability to love and be loved. It is also that place from which flows our character—the ability to trust and bond and the grid, if you will, through which we see and thus respond to all of life.

I want to talk about three layers of our hearts that I think make up a fairly good description or picture of what *agape* may be. The three separate layers are all essential to one another. Together they may give us some understanding of the whole of God's love for us and what we can expect this love to do in our hearts. We will look at three Greek words that have each been translated into the English word *love*. Somehow, I believe the three combine to become one.

One Greek word that is translated *love* is *storge*. *Storge* is what I believe to be the very foundation of the formation of love in our hearts. This word can be defined as "tender affection". It is the bottom layer, if you will, of our foundation. It teaches us intimacy, trust, value, and hope.

Storge

Because *storge* is the first layer of love in our hearts, it would then be apparent that this layer is formed very early in life. Where does this layer find the ingredients of its makings if not from our parents? I believe that it is our parents who are given the role and responsibility to initially pour this love into us and that this process is crucial for the proper, healthy development of one's being.

How do our parents pour *storge* into us? Please understand that when I use the analogy of "pouring into", I am using it as another way of saying "imparting into" or maybe "developing into" the lives of our children. It is, if you will, the pouring in of the essential ingredients necessary and intended by God for us to live the abundant life I believe He wants all of us to live (John 10:10b).

There are three ways our parents help us form this foundational love in our hearts. Remember, as with any building, the foundation must be laid properly and with the correct materials if the building will ever stand up to the test of time. There will always be challenges and storms of life that will blow heavily on this foundation. Thus, proper development of this foundation or the restoration of a foundation poured long ago is crucial!

The first way our parents pour *storge* into us is through ***the voice***. Imagine for a moment, if you can, what it would be like living on the inside of your mother. Without spending a lot of time trying to give scientific examples and proof that a child in the womb can feel or hear, let me just take the liberty and say, **they can . . . do . . . and . . . we did!**

Then one day, in what must have been a very stressful and perhaps frightening process, this child is thrust out of the secure home it had for the last nine months and is taken to a strange new home belonging to its parents. Mom and Dad talk tenderly and lovingly to the baby as they try to show the child their love.

"What a precious little girl you are." "You are so beautiful!" "I love you." "What a handsome boy you are!" "I am so proud of you!" Then, when the baby is crying because of a dirty diaper or because it is hungry, the child might hear something like, "It will be OK, baby; everything is going to be OK." I hope you get the picture.

When a baby hears the tender and affectionate voice of its parents, this is laying a safe and secure foundation in the child's heart. But what if that voice is loud and violent? What if that voice is always negative or critical or abusive? What if it is absent? Then it stands to reason that the foundation is not being laid properly; it is making for a problem later on in the future.

I believe that even when the "voices" we hear as adults are derogatory or are subtly putting us down, this is also very damaging. Years ago when I worked at The Potter's House, a Christian Drug and Alcoholic Rehab center for men in Athens, GA, we had a man there who I will just call David. Rose and I actually lived in our own mobile home that was stationed out on the farm where these 135 men lived.

One day I asked the director if we could have a deck built on the back of the trailer. Knowing David was a carpenter, the director asked David to do it. Now I have built decks for a living myself; I think I know decks, but this one could not compare to anything I could have ever dreamed of building. The detail he used on the railing was beyond my imagination. It was absolutely amazing!

You have to wonder what went wrong for David. Why was he here at this place on a repeat tour and trying to rid himself of his addictions? Well, having known him very well, we had talked about his story. David was the younger of two sons. For some reason, at least to his father, David just could not live up to the standards or achievements of his older brother.

The more and more his dad compared the two boys and chided David because of his apparent shortfall—writing it off to his laziness and lack of drive and ambition—the more David withdrew and started to believe he was not only "no good" but incapable of getting better. Well, with such a long life yet to live, how does someone deal with the prognosis that he or she will "never amount to anything"? So, to mask this brokenness inside, which was spoken over him for years by his dad, David turned to drugs and alcohol to medicate his pain.

Instead of this dad speaking "life" over his son, he was unknowingly speaking death. By the time I met David, he was a young man in his late 20s and was fulfilling the prophecies his dad so many times spoke over him. Parents, please be careful of the words you speak over your children. They might just come to pass!

When my son, Josh, was in the sixth grade, he asked me to speak to his class on careers day . It was during the time I was on the staff of the Potter's House Rehabilitation Center I just mentioned, so I was going to talk to the class about the ills of these vices. As it turned out, one of the coaches I knew walked in the room and heard what I was talking about. Since we were long-time friends, she asked me if I would share these subjects with the school kids who had health class that semester. So, in a two-day period, I spoke to all the middle-school students who that semester had health class. I estimate that in those two days I would have spoken to at least 200 kids.

One of the things I asked every class was this; "Have you ever heard the words, 'You are stupid' or 'You will never amount to anything' or 'Why can't you be like your brother or sister?'" In those two days, fewer than 20 kids did not raise their hands in the affirmative. The majority of these kids were being reared as they heard how bad they were and how they would never amount to anything. Their foundation was being adversely affected, to be sure.

When we hold anger, bitterness, hatred, or unforgiveness within us, the pain of these things, along with the accumulation of all the other potential issues of life, build up and can only be expected eventually to be poured out on someone. Those things deep in our hearts, whether they be good or bad things, will overflow to those around us. As Jesus pointed out, we cannot keep them concealed forever.

> *"Are you still so dull?" Jesus asked them. "Don't you see that whatever enters the mouth goes into the stomach and then out of the body? But the things that come out of the mouth come from the heart, and these make a man unclean. For out of the heart come evil thoughts, murder,*

adultery, sexual immorality, theft, false testimony, slander.
These are what make a man unclean: but eating with un-
washed hands does not make him unclean" (Mt. 15:16-20).

Another way *storge* is poured into us is through **the look**. Have
you ever seen a mother or father holding their little baby as they stare
at that child with a heart full of love and affirmation? As those parents
gaze into the eyes of their child and that child sees those eyes of acceptance, love, and value, *storge* is being poured in. The children are
learning that they are special and valued.

But what if those eyes are filled with a distant stare or even darkness? What if those eyes all the time project anger or fear? What if
those eyes are unable to affirm or value and more often speak of dis-
approval? It stands to reason, then, that this is detrimental to the foundation of that child and that the child will have repercussions later in
life.

I never told any of my sons that I would love them as long as they
received good grades in school. Neither did I ever tell them my love
would extend to them only to the point that they were good and stayed
out of trouble. No parent, hopefully, would ever say such things to
their children. Yet, if they ever came home with poor grades or if they
ever got into any trouble, they received my wrath, which **always** started
with **the look!**

Even now, as adults, we can read much into the way someone's
eyes meet ours. It is not hard to discern such a person's disgust or anger,
especially when you see daggers shooting from his or her eyes. At the
same time, I believe it is possible to see, in many eyes, the genuine love
that flows from a pure, sincere heart. Yes, some people get good at dis-
guises, but the following verse assures us that eventually, they will slip
up.

"The eye is the lamp of the body. If your eyes are good,
your whole body will be full of light. But if your eyes are
bad, your whole body will be full of darkness. If then the

light within you is darkness, how great is that darkness!"
(Mt. 6:22, 23).

Clearly these verses speak not only about the words that we speak to our children and to one another, but I also believe that the eyes also reflect the angry, misguided heart. We have often heard that the eyes are a view into the soul. The eyes cannot help but eventually reflect what is on the inside.

Finally, *storge* is poured into the life of a child through **the touch**. The way we hold children and nurture them through the touch is so important. The touch we, even as adults, experience is very important for the well-being of any of us. Safe touches from a mother and father help bring stability and assurance as well as security to that child.

Recently I was teaching in Pohang, South Korea, at the Good Samaritan Hospital. I was speaking about the Father's Love; my audience consisted of doctors, nurses, and other hospital personnel. It was a bit intimidating, especially as I had no idea I would be doing so until just the day before, but for three evenings I had from 15 to 25 "students".

Whenever I teach on this subject, I always focus on the importance of intimacy being imparted through the touch. This is especially important in Korea, as it is not so common for some parents, especially fathers, to have much intimate contact with their children. I do believe this is changing some with the younger generations coming up, as they have felt the loss of such important touch.

So when I teach this, at some point I always say, "Doctors say that the touch is very important and that from the touch endorphins are released and even some blood cells can begin to reproduce more rapidly . . .." When I started this sentence in front of these doctors, I became startled and stopped as I realized what I was saying and to whom.

Then I asked them whether what I was saying here and teaching wherever I go was correct. Thankfully they assured me that my information was correct. *Whew!* (LOL) So, from the mouth of the professionals, we do find that touch is extremely important. In fact I have heard that for better emotional health each of us needs anywhere from 15 to 20 safe, non-sexual touches a day.

One day years ago my wife and I were listening to someone make this statement. I looked at my wife, who said, "See, I told you that you were supposed to be touching and holding me more!" I smiled, repented, and jokingly immediately began tapping her on her shoulder while I counted to 20. Of course, she let me know instantly that this was not what she or the speaker were referencing. So again, **the touch** is extremely important to our development.

But, what if the touches a child receives at an early age are not safe? What if that touch is inappropriate? What if those touches stem from anger, rage, or frustration? Now, I am in no way suggesting that we do not spank or discipline our children. I believe this can and should be done in a way that is helpful and not harmful. But again, what if the majority of touches a child receives bring fear and pain? You can be sure, this weakens the foundation.

So, as we have seen thus far, the foundation of our hearts are laid at an early age, mainly through *"the voice, the look, and the touch"*. I am calling this foundation the *"storge* type of love". I believe it is vital and necessary to build healthy character, the ability to trust, and the ability to give and receive intimacy. It also helps us to understand proper limits of dependence on others as well as becoming interdependent such as is necessary in any type of community living, whether it be our family, job, or church fellowship.

Even though the word *storge* does not appear in our New Testament, it does not mean that it is not a valid expression of love. It is, however, just the first part of our foundation. Combined, these things will reveal to us perhaps the greatest description of what *agape* really is!

The next layer of our heart, just above the *storge*, is *phileo*. In its various forms this word is translated from the Greek to the English word *love* around 21 times in the New Testament. You might immediately recognize the word since it appears in the name *Philadelphia*, which means the city of brother love.

The word *phileo* has been defined as friendship, loyalty, family, and community, all of which are at their best when immersed in brotherly love. This layer of love can also be defined as tender affection like *storge*, but it is a bit different in that it covers a different level of relationship so to speak. Remember, my purpose here is not to give exact, to-the-letter definitions of words *per se* but only to summarize them to reach our ultimate goal, which is learning what *agape* really is and what it means for us.

I believe *phileo* is helped in its development through what I call "second-level relationships." That is, siblings, grandparents, aunts, uncles, and even friends. In fact, it is this part of our heart that I believe helps us to make and maintain friendships throughout our lives. It is what teaches us how to live and thrive in community relationships, which include those in our eventual jobs.

How well do you get along with people in general? Do you live a guarded or secluded life—perhaps a self-imposed, sheltered life—or are you out there meeting, mingling, and investing in the lives of others around you? Chances are that the answer to these questions reveals how this second level of your heart was developed.

I am 7 and 9 years younger than my two brothers respectively. For the most part we were all together during my formative years. A few years ago I had an interesting experience that helped me at least to understand more about me and my apparent need to develop and maintain long-lasting relationships. Again, this is not at all a scientific understanding but one of a little boy wrapped up in the body of a middle-aged man.

My understanding is that my older brother, Pat, bore quite a bit of the responsibility of taking care of me when I was a baby and in the very early years of my life. My dad, of course, had his job; my mom owned a hair salon. So, Pat, being 9-years older than me, had to change my diapers and at times feed and care for me when my mom was unable to be with me.

There were several things I believe my brother missed out in life as a young teen-ager because in those early years he had a large responsibility in taking care of me. To me, Pat was much more than a brother; he was my "Bubba." I looked up to him; in many ways I guess you could say that he was my idol.

He himself got married at a young age. Even though we always lived in close proximity to him and his family, his busyness with school, a job, and his own family responsibilities brought to me at least a bit of separation anxiety. I always loved and got along with my other brother, Frank; I am sure he participated in caring for me as well, but Pat is the one that I suppose that in my early years had the biggest impact on me.

Several years ago I was struggling through one of those times of discouragement and frustration that I presume most of us go through in life. Since by then both of my parents had been deceased for some time, I began to feel such a strong desire and need for a more intimate relationship with my two brothers.

One day while I was praying, it hit me like a ton of bricks. For the first time in my life I realized that I was viewing my older brother more like a dad than as a brother. I guess there could be something to be said about the fact that he is the elder brother and that the three of us are the only remaining links to our mom and dad. Maybe some of what I was feeling was that, but I think it went much deeper.

As one who basically stood in as a parent during those early years, my brother poured into me, I believe, more on the *storge* level than on the *phileo*. When you add to that the fact that both brothers were a bit older and of course got busy with their own growing-up years, I think that maybe I missed some of the *phileo* input that I probably needed.

So for most of my married life I have felt a big need for intimate input and fellowship from long-lasting, close friendships. I have many friends but only a few I would say have been around for years and could be considered intimate, call-on-anytime friends. Thank God Jesus said He considers us friends! (John 15:13-15).

I remember shortly after having this revelation concerning my brother Pat that I called him to tell him what I was feeling. He was just getting off a plane after a business trip. The few minutes we shared in that conversation were both emotional and priceless! Today, I enjoy a wonderful relationship with both of my brothers. Their own deep spirituality has helped me tremendously on my personal journey. God has had His hand on all three of us and is using us all in a special way to influence the world around us.

Finally, the third layer of the heart is the Greek word *eros*. This word also does not appear in the New Testament, but again, I still believe it is a vital part of the makeup of the heart. *Eros* speaks of passionate love. It is romantic love that can be, but is not necessarily, sexual. As much as I feel that *storge* and *phileo* are vital and necessary components of our hearts and are important for our personal wholeness, I believe that *eros* is equally as important!

This level was intended to be at its best when developed and nurtured between a husband and wife. Because of the romantic and potential sexual characteristics of *eros,* I want to give an illustration here that, I must forewarn you, is of a mature, adult context. So, please be advised.

There is during the sexual relationship and experience between a husband and wife a few moments in which nothing else in the world seems to matter, you feel at complete, unexplainable peace, and you experience unbelievable joy and happiness.

Remember again that we are building up to something here. The three layers of love that I am describing are revealing a part of who we are. I strongly believe that the understanding of their workings within us will lead us into a greater revelation of what *agape* is in our lives. Since the word *agape* is used so often in the New Testament, I am convinced that it is vital for us to understand what it means and how it actually applies to us. Later in this analogy the description I just shared in the context of *eros* will have a greater meaning.

So in brief, we have seen three levels of the heart that are perhaps the major contributors to the healthy development and well-being of our lives. Again, *storge* is poured into us through our parents; *phileo* is poured into us by second-level relationships in our lives such as those with brothers and sisters; and *eros* is best developed between husband and wife.

It is my opinion that every human being has broken *storge* and that it all started the moment Adam and Eve were put out of the Garden.

> ***So the Lord God banished him from the Garden of Eden to work the ground from which he had been taken. After he drove the man out, he placed on the east side of the Garden of Eden cherubim and a flaming sword flashing back and forth to guard the way to the tree of life***
> (Gen. 3:23, 24).

In the Garden, Adam and Eve would have fully experienced and lived in the love of God. They would have been completely whole— spirit, mind, and body—because of this amazing love. They would have known complete peace, joy, rest, affirmation, and safety all because of the love of the One we call Father. The moment they were put outside of this love, they became the first human orphans. Their hearts—the foundation within them—would have been broken!

When Christ came to die for the sins of man, it was far more than a kind gesture from a compassionate God to keep us out of hell! Thank God for that benefit for sure, but far greater was a much-overlooked and misunderstood benefit. You see, since that day when the first man was put out of the Garden, the Father was forced to keep somewhat of a distance between Himself and man.

It was not because He didn't love man anymore; this occurred simply because He was so holy. If sinful man ever got too close to His holiness, man would instantly die forever. We must understand here that this "love at a distance" was sad for mankind but heart wrenching for God! So Christ's sacrifice on the Cross provided a way for the Father to come to us and again enjoy the love relationship He so enjoys (John 14:6).

There is a natural and not so good progression that takes place when the pains of broken *storge* finally kick in—and believe me, it will, sooner or later. Without knowing when the transition takes place, the brokenness of our first layer in our foundation will necessarily lead us to looking to compensate in the second layer, *phileo*.

It is at this time we might find ourselves "hanging out" with folks we normally would never associate with, going places we would never go, and doing things we would never do. Something else that seems mighty suspect to me as being an attempt to fix *storge* with *phileo* is when people are so immersed in their careers that there is no time for anything or anyone else but that career. Loving parents whose jobs keep them from the family will ease their consciences by thinking they are "providing" for their families.

This can be an unconscious attempt on our part to medicate the pain of brokenness inside. Sure you might get wealthy and famous working 12 to 16 hours a day, but is it really worth the emptiness many of these people really feel inside or worth the loss of your family? In the case of the family, basically, you are just passing the brokenness you received on to the next generation; on and on it goes.

Let me just say it again. In my humble opinion, no amount of *phileo* can fix or compensate for broken *storge*. Oh, there may be some temporary relief for a while. Some people may be able to live the rest of their lives with this "robbing Peter to pay Paul" syndrome, so to speak, but what is more important is being able to live a life of peace and rest.

In April 2006, when Rose and I first went to South Korea to teach at an YWAM BEDTS school on the Father's Heart, we saw something that at first we were not expecting. Everywhere we went in public, we saw women holding hands, walking with arms around each other's waist, or holding on to each other in some way.

That first trip we also saw five sets of men doing the same. You can tell by the mere fact that I can tell you an exact number here that it had a profound effect on us. As far as the women were concerned, we quickly discerned that this was not anything but a display of genuine love and affection between two people. To be honest, where the men were concerned, it took a little longer to arrive at the same conclusion!

As the Lord was showing me this picture of the three layers of the heart and how it was a picture of His love restoring us, I believe He also showed me what I believe is a profound explanation of what I have just described. My theory is that what I was seeing in Korea was an attempt by an entire culture to fix or at least compensate for what I believed obviously was broken *storge*.

At least in older generations the Korean father was not very affectionate, often distant, and more-than-likely very authoritarian to both children and wife. I am not criticizing here by any means but simply making an observation, for which I have received plenty of affirmative responses when I ask Koreans about their fathers.

I believe that in many ways an issue still exists in this regard, as there is so much competition in Korea. These are some of the most intelligent, hard-working people in the world, but the competition is horrendous. To keep your edge, so to speak, in the work force, long hours and sometimes compromising gestures are required. In short, while fathers may be getting a little more touchy-feely, I don't know if they are home enough to do so or if they have the energy when they are.

I really believe that all of the touching and affection shown to one another may be an attempt at using *phileo* to repair or at best ease the pain of the broken *storge* in people's lives. In one respect, if I am anywhere near correct, I thank God for the substitute. For some, it may be enough to get them through this life, albeit limping all the way.

I don't want to sound too redundant, but I really want to paint a picture here that encourages us to run to the Father. I believe for most of us, it is only natural to reach out on a horizontal plane to get what only Daddy can give us. It is mostly our misguided attempt to fix one part of our broken foundation with another part that is perhaps equally broken. Besides that, you just cannot fix *storge* with *phileo;* they are two different parts of a whole.

What happens to someone who is drawing from *phileo* to fix *storge* and it doesn't work? It never will work, at least not long-term. I think when we come up short in our efforts, there is only one other place to go to try to repair or replace the broken foundation of *storge*; I believe it is *eros*. I strongly believe that this is the reason we have such an immorality problem in this world. Too many of us are looking for love in all the wrong places!

Eros is at its best when it comes from the health, purity, and strength of the rest of our hearts— *storge* and *phileo*. In other words, this may be the top of the volcano, so to speak; what emerges from this is determined by the rumblings beneath.

Remember, *eros* speaks of "passion" and "romance"— two powerful emotions that have their benefits in both the natural and spirit world.

As can be expected, both can be abused, misused, or at best, misguided. When we have the comfort, security, and warmth of the other parts of our hearts, our expression of passion and romance will be at its most pure, and may I say, most effective and fulfilling state.

In truth, while in my opinion these three layers of love make up the heart, each has its own place and function. Neither of them can repair nor replace another. Like an arm or a leg, both are vital in their function, but neither can really replace the other very effectively.

So, here is an amazing analogy. In the Father's love, every day our Parent, the Father, comes to us in quiet intimacy and restores the broken *storge* in our hearts. Through the Word of God we clearly hear His *voice* gently speaking to us, His *eyes/gaze/look* firmly fixed on us, and His *supernatural touch* restoring and resting upon us. Wow!

In this analogy I am not trying to dissect God here, but for the sake of the illustration, I want to emphasize the potential role each part of the Godhead can play in our lives. And just to be clear yet again, when I say "in the Father's love", I am not talking about the intellectual assent and knowledge of the God who loves us. The Father never intended nor could He ever be content alone with our head-knowledge of Him. Neither could we ever receive the full benefit of being a son or daughter of the God of the universe with head-knowledge alone.

No, I am talking about an experiential knowledge of Almighty God, our Father—yeah, our Daddy. By this knowledge I am talking about a daily personal and intimate fellowship with the One who first called us *sons* and *daughters*. This is the same One who sent His only begotten Son to die for us so that we could not only be sons and daughters but heirs of His Throne (Rom. 8:17).

He is the same One who talked face to face with Moses (Ex. 33:11). He is the One who promised Joshua He would never leave him and told him to be strong and courageous (Josh. 1:6, 5). And our Daddy is the One who is captivated by our hearts like Boaz was with Ruth (Ruth 3:9-11) and who has chosen us over all of creation to be His and His alone like the king did with Esther (Esther 2:17-18).

If we ever hope to enjoy to the fullest this intimacy with our Father, we must adopt a similar attitude to that of Esther. She sought the Person of the King over the privilege of the Palace. In other words, she wanted the King more than she wanted the kingdom. She desired relationship more than rewards.

We must look to and trust in our God like Solomon did when his God simply said, *"Ask for whatever you want me to give you"* (2 Chron. 1:7). To this open-ended question, most of us would immediately search for that shopping list we always keep somewhere nearby for such a time as this. No, like Solomon, this is not a time to ask for our desires to be fulfilled but for what we know would please Him most.

When we seek Him more than seeking what He can give us, I believe we will hear Him whisper into our hearts something like,

> *". . . since this is your heart's desire and you have not asked for wealth, riches or honor, nor for the death of your enemies, and since you have not asked for a long life but for wisdom and knowledge to govern my people over whom I have made you king, therefore wisdom and knowledge will be given you. And, I will also give you wealth, riches and honor, such as no king who was before you ever had and none after you will have"* (2 Chron. 1:11-12).

So then, when this Father of ours comes to us in intimacy and we are participants in and recipients of this love, I believe that He is pouring healing into our broken *storge*. This, my dear friend, is what He longs to do for you and for me. You might say His greatest joy is to be the steward of our hearts!

Then, every day, the Son, our Brother (John 1:12-13) and Friend (John 15:14-15) ministers healing, restoration, and refreshing to our damaged *phileo*. It is through the daily fellowship with the Son that we are able to love with the love that He commands. The importance of this ability to love others is seen in the following verses and can occur only, I believe, once the *storge* and *phileo* are restored.

> *"A new command I give you: Love* (agape) *one another. As I have loved* (agape) *you, so you must love* (agape) *one another. By this all men will know that you are my disciples, if you love* (agape) *one another"* (John 13:34-35).

Finally, every day, the Holy Spirit, along with Jesus our Bridegroom, in romantic and passionate fashion, restores and aligns this part of our heart to its intended purpose. ***How great is the love*** (agape) ***the Father has lavished on us, that we should be called children of God! And that is what we are . . .*** (1 John 3:1).

It is only when this part of our heart is at its best with God that it can fully and completely mesh with our spouse's heart. I am talking far more here than sex with our spouses. I am talking about a genuine, complete, and fulfilling relationship between us. When our hearts are in right standing with and daily touched by our God, what pours out from us to our spouses, family, friends, and our world can't help but be a blessing.

Now, I understand that the verses above, when they use the word *love,* speak of *agape.* My point again is to bring us to a greater understanding of what *agape* is and how we realize it the most. But it is here that I want to share with you perhaps the most wonderful part of the Spirit of God's ministering to us.

There is a place in the Holy Spirit where nothing else in the world seems to matter, where you feel at complete, unexplainable peace, and where you experience unbelievable joy and happiness! While it is true most of us have felt this only on occasion, I assure you that it is an experience that He wants us to enjoy every day.

To sum it all up now, the Love our Father has for us every day is at work in our hearts—that *storge, phileo,* and *eros* within—restoring it to its intended function. As we begin to live in and enjoy this inti-

macy with Him, then we can truly fulfill Jesus' command as given to
the Pharisees to love (*agape*).

" . . . Love the Lord your God with all your heart
and with all your soul and with all your mind.
This is the first and greatest commandment.
And the second is like it: Love your neighbor
as yourself. All the Law and the Prophets hang on these
two commandments" (Mt.22:37-40).

AGAPE

Eros
Phileo
Storge

Chapter 10

Substitutes

All of my life I have struggled with my weight. I remember that as a young teen-ager when I was home alone during those periods between getting home from school and when my dad would get home from work, I felt the intense need or desire for something to eat. My parents always provided well for me; we always had plenty of food to eat in the house, but during those *alone times*, something just seemed to take over any control I might have had back then.

Summertime and the holidays were the worst. When I would be home alone as my parents were at work, I can remember getting out slices of bread and putting huge chunks of butter on them and then putting them into the oven for a few minutes. I can still smell the toasted bread and taste that buttery taste. When this wasn't good enough, I had to get imaginative.

Toasting bread slices in the oven and putting gobs of ketchup on them was another favorite. Of course doing the same with slices of cheese would have been another option. Then there was the rummaging through the refrigerator to find anything I could to satisfy this "need" for food.

Shopping with my mom, while not the normal enjoyable pastime for a teen-ager, was for me an interesting adventure. My mom and I both loved a particular brand of nacho chips. Many times when we first got into the store and secured our shopping cart, we went directly for the chips.

Normally, first thing, my mom would get two bags of our favorite brand off the shelf. One, to go home with us, went in the cart; the other was for our enjoyment as we walked around the store. I still remember the strange look on the cashier's face as my mom always put the empty bag up on the counter along with the other groceries so she could be charged for our shopping delicacy.

Another favorite for me was Nestles Chocolate. We almost always had a can of this around the house; I loved to add a little milk to my chocolate mix (LOL). I knew of nothing better than a large glass of cold chocolate milk. In fact, as a child living in Hempstead, Long Island, I remember my dad often stopping at the drive-through dairy after church on Sundays to buy us a half-gallon or so of ice-cold chocolate milk.

From an early age it seemed like I was destined to be the biggest Mercardante in the family. Coming from an Italian family we all loved to eat; as I grew into those teen years, I could sure eat. It almost seemed that there was a little pride from my dad as his youngest son was growing up (and out). What seemed great at the time for me and perhaps a bit of pride for my dad later proved to be a big issue (pardon the pun) for me.

By the time I was in the 10th grade, I surpassed my dad and rivaled my two older brothers as far as size went. I was involved in sports, so I was pretty active and in great shape. Weight never seemed to be an issue. When I played football in high school, I weighed around 225, but it seemed to fit well with my almost six-foot frame.

Then I got married. My wife, Rose, was reared by an Italian mother who loved to cook. My mother-in-law would make all of the Italian things that I was reared around. From an early age Rose learned how to cook these foods as well. So, during my first year of marriage I gained 50 pounds. I attributed it to my wife's great cooking. Hey, I guess I can blame this all on her . . ..

Still, during those first few years it didn't seem to be much of a problem, because I remained active. I worked out in the gym and still lifted weights for a while. But as you can imagine, it wasn't long before the busyness of life overtook my desire and energy to go to the gym; the rest is history. With seemingly no notice my chest just slipped to my waist!

Now let's fast-forward 35 years and try to do a little math work. Without much effort I can probably account for somewhere between 500 to 750 pounds that I have lost during this time. Like a yo-yo the weight went up and down, up and down, and up and down again until it just stayed up . . . or down, if you consider location.

I always wore clothes that I thought would hide the weight problem, but I understand now that there was little hope of ever accomplishing that goal. I was constantly embarrassed and ashamed, yet I continued to eat myself sick. I have started probably a hundred or so diets, made countless resolutions, and waited for endless Mondays to arrive so I could start all over again.

I began to look at things a little differently, however, when we began to hear the message about how much the Father loved us. We heard that the Father really loved us without any hooks or conditions. We were told that there was nothing that we could do to get Him to love us any more than He already did and that there was nothing we could do to get Him to love us less.

This unfolding revelation of the Father's love did not help me to lose weight, but it did set me free from a lot of the shame. Now, I would allow myself to be seen in public with a pullover shirt rather than the normal, oversized button-up shirts that I always wore with a

T-shirt under it. I wasn't so paranoid when I would notice someone's lingering glance that I felt sure was a look of condemnation and mockery.

I was slowly starting to love myself for who God made me to be. I understood that He didn't make me fat, but just knowing that He loved me regardless of whether I was fat or skinny, tall or short, seemed to bring me some comfort. When I first realized that some of the great preachers of the past, such as H.A. Ironside or Charles Spurgeon, were a little portly, I felt less and less guilt and shame.

Yes, I was justifying my problem with food by comparing myself to others, but be that as it may, when I would think of these men from the past or see some of the modern greats that were a bit overweight, I just felt like it was who I would always be. I admit I was a bit saddened when T.D. Jakes lost all of his weight. (LOL)

I will never forget an incident at a small church we attended years ago while we lived in San Diego, CA. The pastor had a tremendous gift of healing. His dad was on staff as well. It just seemed as if the Spirit of God was alive and powerful in this church. He was! The pastor, however, was very overweight.

This was no problem for me, of course, and I am sure most of the folks in this church didn't mind having a super-sized pastor as long as the Spirit of God kept moving through him. Well, one day Brother Denny was all fired up in his message; the particular point he was trying to get across was about the evils of smoking.

Then it happened. Right there in the middle of the sermon, in front of God and everyone, a young man that could have passed for a "hippie" stood up and yelled at the pastor. "Preacher, when you get that spoon out of your mouth, I'll get the cigarette out of my mouth!" And then he sat down.

Frankly, I don't remember the response from the pastor when that happened, but at the time there was a deafening silence. The impact of what that boy said has remained with me all these years later. It reminds me of another story that I have heard is a true story, although I cannot verify it.

Apparently H. A. Ironside was near to the home of the great revivalist preacher/pastor Charles Spurgeon. Wanting to meet this great man of God who left his hearers overwhelmed with his anointed preaching, Ironside decided to stop by the home and meet this mighty man of God.

Well it seemed that Spurgeon was a big man himself just like Ironside, with one major exception. Spurgeon was reported to have often smoked a cigar. When Ironside knocked on the door and Spurgeon answered with a large stogie in his mouth, Ironside was taken back. Before he could think, he spurted out something like, "I can't believe you smoke cigars!"

Being a man of quick response and wit, Spurgeon reached out his hand, tapped Ironside's belly, and said, "I can't believe you have such a large belly!" This says much about our obsession with other people's problems or habits with little thought to the things that may plague us.

During our first ministry trip to Seoul, Korea, I was invited by two of my Western counterparts to go to a bathhouse. Up until that point in my life I had only heard some of the negative things that apparently had happened in similar places around the States, so I was a bit skeptical. Being persuaded by both these very godly men that this was a "must-do" thing when you were in Korea, I went.

I was prepared to enter this adventure with my gym shorts on, but, no, no, this is not the way you do it! It was truly back to nature in this place. So, in the spirit of cooperation and adventure, in I went. Well, as you can imagine, I would have been the largest human being most Koreans have ever seen other than perhaps in Western Movies or the occasional statue of Buddha.

Keep in mind that in a place like this, nothing is sacred or hidden. I can remember one incident that happened that brings me almost to tears of laughter as I think about it. I was taking my shower in front of the mirror that was there. As I was looking into the mirror and was washing, a young Korean boy went running past me.

As he was running by, he casually turned his head my way. All of a sudden I could see him do a double-take and at the same time put on the brakes as he completely halted. "Ohhhhh," was all that emerged from his mouth at the time (funny, that word must be universal). Then I saw him signal his little buddy to come and see this unbelievable sight. Of course when he arrived, they both just couldn't help but giggle. GREAT!

Eating for comfort is not the only "crutch" or "substitute" some people use. When you add into the mix such things as drugs, alcohol, pornography, and even the self-absorbed "I need to look beautiful" addiction, you can see that as a nation we have some real problems. I might add that this is not only a problem here in the U.S. Wherever you look around this world, you will find people doing different things to medicate their inner pain. The particular "action" may be different, but the desired results are the same . . . comfort!

I want you to stop for a few minutes and really think about those things you are using or doing in life right now that are only medicating the real hurt inside. Be honest with yourself. I believe that many of the things we excuse as just a "bad habit" or our "drive for success", if looked at honestly, are little more that our attempt at cooling the fire that burns within.

What are you substituting for the unconditional, life-giving, healing power of God's love? If you are like me, by now you are sick and tired of being sick and tired and ready for a change. Do you remember the often-used definition of *insanity*? It is trying the same thing over and over again and expecting different results. In fact, change will never happen that way, no matter how hard we butt our heads against that brick wall! The good news is that there is hope. Paul knew this when he wrote to the church at Ephesus.

Now to him who is able to do immeasurably more than all we ask or imagine, according to his power that is at work within us, to him be glory in the church and in Christ Jesus throughout all generations, forever and ever! Amen (Eph. 3:20, 21).

So I give to you the same comfort that I have received through the healing, restoration, deliverance, and encouragement that my Heavenly Father has worked through me thus far. Be comforted to know, my dear brother and sister, that Papa is still on the Throne. He is looking after you. He alone is the medicine we need in our lives; no other substitute will do!

Today I have not completely conquered the weight problem and seem to wrestle with it constantly. It has been the topic of much discussion between Papa and me, but this one thing I know: He can and will hold me and carry me when the weight of this world overwhelms me. He will do the same for you.

Chapter 11

The Cycle of Pain

Have you ever noticed how much of life seems to go in cycles? Clothes that may have been out of style for many years, if you can afford the room to hold on to them, are likely to return someday. The financial markets seem to also go through cycles. Granted, some seem like they are far worse than others, but nonetheless, they are cycles indeed.

At the Christian Rehabilitation center that I mentioned earlier, we would house as many as 135 men who were involved in what I felt was a very good program designed not just to keep them from drugs and alcohol but to free them from the deadly hold these things had on their lives. One of the classes I taught at the time had to do with the many different cycles of life we all seem to go through.

For example in one class I would draw on the board a picture of one cycle that many marriages go through. At the top of the cycle was the honeymoon stage where everything was lovely, peaceful, and calm. As you continued in the cycle, I would note how eventually there would be a buildup of stress and pressure that would increase as life went on.

Then, at some point there was a blowup. You know, those knock-down, drag-outs we sometimes experience as husbands and wives (or so I have been told). Finally, as we kept going in our cycle, there would be the releasing of the pressure after the blowup. This would lead to the honeymoon stage again. Then the cycle just continued.

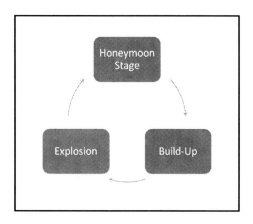

When Rose and I first began to hear the life-changing message of God's unconditional love for us, it began to free us from much of the pain and shame of our pasts. We soon began to realize, however, that this was not just a one-time experience, class, or seminar we were attending, but it was a life change we were learning.

The fear I have for so many today is that they will read a book or go to a school or seminar on the Father's Love and then walk away thinking they got it! That is the reason I wrote the chapter called "This Is Truth". It really stemmed from an experience Rose and I had in Busan, South Korea, in 2006.

We were teaching at the first-ever Father's Heart School in Korea. This group is now hosted by an amazing group of people in Busan— Grace, Pastor Joon-il, and Pastor Jun. Their hearts' desire to see people in Korea freed from the hurts and wounds of their past and walking in the freedom of Daddy's love is unmatched. They are pioneers of such a great work there.

This first school was in part a memorial to Jack Winter. He was a man who was known affectionately by some as "Mr. Korea". He had gone to Korea 40 times in his lifetime to minister on the Father's love. He and his wife, Dorothy, were not only used by God to pioneer the message of the Father's love 40 years ago but were carriers of this love as well!

Now, God has always loved us and always will. But what I mean when I say that Jack Winter was a pioneer is that God used him to birth this amazing revelation of this love to many people in this world. Jack had an amazing anointing and boldness to see and then say things about the Father's love that seemed to unlock tremendous peace and rest in people.

In 2000 Jack spent four days in our home while he taught at our small church. I may have the distinction of being the only person in the world who would dare to take this world-renowned, mighty man of God to eat at a Waffle House Restaurant, a well-known chain here in Georgia where I presently live. Actually, it was the love and grace of our Father flowing through him that made this a distinction he would never have shared with anyone else, just to protect me! (LOL)

For me, and I am sure for my good friend, Vic Pesaresi, who was with us that day, there was something about Jack that set him apart. I remember sitting at our dinner table one night and just staring at him and praying, "Father, why couldn't I have met this man 20 years ago?" When Rose and I took Jack that last day to his next venue, on the way home I told Rose to wait before she washed his bed sheets.

So, what I am about to say will sound crazy, but it happened, OK? When I got home, the first thing I did was to lie in that bed for a while and pray that God would transfer onto me some of Jack's anointing and the revelation he carried. I know it may seem like it, but I was not really putting this brother on a pedestal; I simply was desperate to know the love from the Father he carried.

Well, did it work? Did lying in that bed and praying for more of what Jack had have any effect on my life? When this experience happened back in 2000, up until that point in my life I probably had not said the word *Korea* or *Koreans* more than 50 times. In April 2006, Rose and I made our first trip to Seoul, Korea. Since then, I have been to Korea 19 times to more than 18 different cities as I taught on the Father's Love! You make the call!

Anyway, while we were there in 2006, a pastor and his wife took Rose and me out for an amazing meal—far greater than something you would get at the Waffle House, I assure you. It was during conversation that night that we were asked a question that still breaks my heart when I think about it. I can't seem to get it out of my mind.

This dear pastor's wife said that in 1984 (22 years earlier), Jack Winter traveled to Korea; she and her husband attended the meetings. Sometime during that meeting, in typical Jack protocol, he embraced her and prayed this simple prayer, just as he had prayed before with multiple thousands around the world.

He said, "Father, may my hands become your hands, and may my arms become your arms, and would you fill this woman with your love tonight?" As this dear woman recounted the experience—one that both Rose and I had also experienced ourselves from Jack—there seemed to be mixed emotions in her eyes. There was a sense of joy, mixed with sorrow, with occasional periods of hope shining through. Then she asked me this question that I will always remember.

"That night, when Jack held me and prayed that I would be filled with the Father's love, did I get it?" Even as I write this, I am immediately taken back to that night as if it happened yesterday. What I can't shake is this. For 22 years up to that night, this precious saint of God was not sure if she had received the Father's love in her life!

Can I shout it from the housetops once again for all to hear? YES, YES, YES, HE LOVES YOU NOW. HE ALWAYS HAS. HE AL-

WAYS WILL. As I mentioned in a previous chapter, the problem is not with His giving but with our receiving. Any wall, whether real or perceived, between Him and you today is a wall of your making, not His.

When Jesus died on the cross, it was not just to keep us out of hell but to open the way for the Father to run to us with open arms and to enjoy the intimacy that He has always wanted with us (John 14:6). What necessarily had to stop after sin entered the world (intimacy) was resumed through the life, death, and resurrection of Jesus Christ, the only begotten Son of God. It was resumed, that is, to the level of our understanding, believing, and receiving this truth!

Early in our relationship with Jack and Trisha Frost and Shiloh Place Ministries, we were taught about a continuing "cycle" that we go through and that can only be broken by embracing as sons and daughters the love of the Father. This teaching has now become one of the messages I always teach wherever I go, if time permits. In Korea, it seems to be one of the most impacting. I want to share it with you. We call it "the Cycle of Pain".

We are going to look at the five different stages of this cycle. This cycle starts with the wounded heart within us—you could say, the broken *storge*. This brokenness produces an inevitable love deficit that leads us in a progression around the cycle and leading back again to more brokenness and wounding. From there the cycle just continues spinning out of control throughout our lives—that is, until we begin to receive the healing balm of the Father's love penetrating deep within our hearts and bringing us wholeness.

The Wound

There are many things in life that cause us deep wounding; the effect they can have on our lives can be devastating. People say or do things to us or don't say and do what they should. It is in those earliest, most formative years, as mentioned in a previous chapter, that many

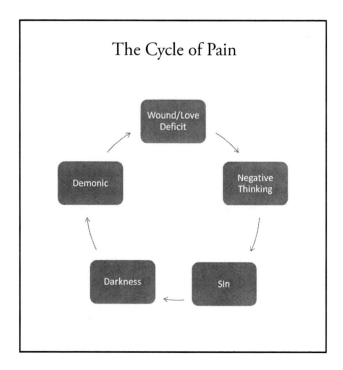

of these wounds find their beginning. Even now, there is every opportunity to have someone or something cause wounding.

> *A cheerful heart is good medicine, but a crushed spirit*
> *dries up the bones. A man's spirit sustains him in sickness.*
> *But a crushed spirit who can bear?*
> (Prov. 17:22 and 18:14).

These wounds are like a crushing in our hearts that will leave us weak and weary. If we do not do anything about them, they may hinder us from fulfilling the full destiny God has planned for us. Certainly, if they are left unchecked, we will lack the fullness of joy and peace that is available to us through Christ (John 16:33).

These wounds are like a root that goes deep within our core being and affects everything we do and everyone with whom we interact.

Our emotional strength will be weakened, our prayer life and intimacy with God will not be what it could, and our walk in this life will be marred with many slips, trips, and falls. When you add to this the fact that we can only give away what we have, it is easy to see that we are too often just duplicating ourselves in the lives of those we influence.

Therefore, strengthen your feeble arms and weak knees. Make level paths for your feet, so that the lame may not be disabled, but rather healed. Make every effort to live in peace with all men and to be holy; without holiness no one will see the Lord. See to it that no one misses the grace of God and that no bitter root grows up to cause trouble and defile many (Heb. 12:12-15).

The bitter root that can be deep inside of us will not only spoil things for you, but sadly, it will affect and scar those around you (Mt. 15:16-20). The wounding we feel, often the results of this bitter root, will leave us with a love deficit. In other words, we will be deficient in the full level of love we are supposed to have; that was determined by God before the foundation of the world.

I will not go into a long look into the how's and why's of wounding, but reading through my story as I have shared it with you will give you a fairly good idea of many of the causes. I remember our first conference with Shiloh Place when we heard about some 19 potential causes of wounding in our lives.

After that session, when Rose and I went back to our room, we were ready to give up! Of the 19 potential causes of wounding, I could relate personally to all 19 and Rose to 18. Needless to say, we were overwhelmed and felt hopeless. The good news, however, is that God is in the restoration business; here we are as a testimony to that fact. We learned that you have to take things one step, one day at a time. **Father, may we learn to live and find our sustenance from the daily bread you offer us.**

Negative Thinking

The wounding in our lives creates within us a grid by which we see and experience life. They help us to form strong opinions about ourselves—opinions that may or may not be true. Why do you think you are unattractive? Where did you get the idea that you are not intelligent enough to excel in learning? How did you reach the conclusion that you would never amount to anything?

These wounds, along with many other negative thoughts and actions, at an early age helped shape us. Because of things that were said or done to us, we arrived at a conclusion about ourselves that left such an impression in us that we eventually began to believe the lies.

For myself, because much of my early years seemed to be dominated by a woman who I felt I could never please, I learned (negative thinking) that I could never please women. So, the way this acted out in me was that I lived a life of trying to go overboard to receive love and approval from women. Even though I seemed to have unconditional love from my dear wife, since my mindset was that home was not a safe place, I could not receive much of her love.

Take for example **a little girl** that is never held or cuddled by her daddy. For whatever reason, Daddy just couldn't or wouldn't hold her, speak words of love and affirmation over her, and ingrain into her *(storge)* that she was beautiful, special, wanted, and needed. After the many attempts by this little girl to get from daddy what he is supposed to be giving her, she finally one day reaches the devastating conclusion that she isn't pretty, lovable, or desirable. She grows up seeing herself from that viewpoint and believes that the world sees her that way, too.

Once these negative thoughts about ourselves take root, it is extremely hard, apart from a genuine and personal revelation of God's love for us, to believe anything different. No matter how many times her husband may say she is beautiful, special, or attractive to him, she will just not be able to see or feel it.

Years ago in our church Rose had a very interesting experience. When the service was over, for whatever reason Rose was standing near the front and watched and listened as this event unfolded. Two women in the church who were standing about 30-feet apart suddenly started walking toward each other to speak. One of the women was attractive and the other was highly attractive. (Surely I can't offend anyone with that one.) When they reached each other, the pretty woman said immediately to the very pretty woman, "I wish I was as pretty as you!" Rose watched in amazement as the highly attractive woman blurted out with all the sincerity of her heart, "Oh, I wish I was as pretty as you!"

Both women had such a negative view of themselves, it didn't matter how pretty either of them was; they could never see it. I suspect many of the high-dollar, beautiful models we see in fashion magazines and some of the beautiful actresses on the television would feel the same way about themselves. I believe that for some, their lifestyle proves me right.

So again, our impression or view of ourselves and our negative thinking dominate our lives and become the grid by which we react to everything in life. Fortunately, there is hope, as we will see a little later.

Sin

Remember, we are looking at a cycle here. We started with "the wound" and learned that it helped form in us a devastating self-image of ourselves; here we are calling that image *negative thinking*. The problem is that negative thinking will most always lead to "sin". This sin will be the result of our looking for love in all the wrong places.

You see, when we believe a lie about ourselves, we begin a journey through life to find someone or something that will tell us this lie is just that—a lie. We might go from person to person, school to school, business to business, church to church, or one adventure to another just to find the love we are so desperately missing.

The problem is that some of the things we may begin doing are sin. Regardless of the "why" behind our journey of looking for love and affirmation, sin is sin. There is just no way around this fact. Usually we realize this after the first attempt or two of searching for this love in these wrong places, but with the pain being so intense inside us and our need intensifying to find something or someone who will disprove what we believe about ourselves, we just continue.

For me, my need for approval from women led me to sometimes overlook their issues. Instead of my being the pastor/watchman I should have been, I simply gave many a pass. Instead of being the spiritual leader God had made me to be, I often became a follower, if doing so meant getting their approval and affirmation.

For the little girl mentioned above, she can be assured that one day some little boy will tell her whatever she wants or needs to hear to get whatever he wants. Regardless of how strong she might be spiritually, eventually, it is very possible she will give in to the pain and take the temporary fix she is being offered. When she finds out it is temporary, guilt and shame only intensify her wounds.

Darkness

One problem with sin is that for most of us, we feel compelled to hide the sins we have committed. We know what we did or are still doing is wrong, yet we fear what people might think if they ever found out the truth about us. For most of us, even though we are conscious that sin is sin, we fear what the repercussions might be from man more than we do from God.

We understand that Jesus is the "*light*" of the world, in that He came to expose sin and darkness and to show us another "*way*" (John 14:6). The way of our enemy, Satan, is directly opposed to this "*way*" of Christ. Because of the nature of evil, such as lying and deception, which in and of themselves are things which keep out the "*light*" (truth) and promote falsehood (darkness), the obvious distinction between Christ and Satan are clear (Rom. 1:19-20).

When Jesus came to the conclusion of His 40 days of fasting and prayer in the wilderness, He returned to Galilee. Listen to the account of His entering into this new phase of His life and ministry and the quote He uses from Isaiah 9:2.

> *"When Jesus heard that John had been put in prison, he returned to Galilee. Leaving Nazareth, he went and lived in Capernaum, which was by the lake in the area of Zebulun and Naphtali—to fulfill what was said through the prophet Isaiah: Land of Zebulun and land of Naphtali, the way to the sea, along the Jordan, Galilee of the Gentiles – <u>the people living in darkness have seen a great light; in the land of the shadow of death light has dawned</u>"*
> (Mt. 4:12-16, emphasis mine).

Jesus, the Light, was sent to expose darkness. As a side note it is interesting to notice that Jesus actually changed one word in His quote of Isaiah. Isaiah said that the people "*walked*", or as the NIV renders it, were "*walking in darkness*". The editors of the NIV change the wording in Matthew to say "*living in darkness*".

The KJV and other interpretations, however, quote Isaiah as saying "*walked*" and Jesus using the word "*sat*". I mention this only to emphasize what I think Jesus may have been alluding to at the time. That was that things had gotten a whole lot worse in His day than they were in Isaiah's. To Isaiah, people "*walked*" or were walking through darkness. These words, in and of themselves, can offer a possible hope that they would one day walk out of the darkness. Jesus however was saying that the people just sat down in the darkness, as if to stay! Either way, darkness had become a lifestyle to people.

On the other hand, those of us who name the Name of Christ as our Lord and Savior neither walk, sit, nor stay in darkness. He made it clear when He declared,

> *"You are the light of the world. A city on a hill cannot be hidden. Neither do people light a lamp and put it under a bowl. Instead they put it on a stand, and it gives light to everyone in the house. In the same way, let your light shine before men, that they may see your good deeds and praise your Father in heaven."* (Matthew 5:14-16).

Unfortunately, there are too many people in the Body of Christ today that resemble far too closely the **teachers of the law and the Pharisees.** According to the account in John 8:1-11, these religious guys were trying to find a basis to accuse Jesus of not being who He said He was. So, they caught a woman in the act of adultery and brought her not only to Jesus, but they **made her stand before the group.**

Here is my point. Regardless of the underlying motives behind their actions, many people enjoy "exposing" people who sin. In some warped way we feel that by exposing someone else's faults, it might take the light off of our own. We seem to forget that sin is sin is sin.

So, when we do sin, we have to hide those sins in darkness. Because of all the "what-if's" that could be if people found out that we did a particular thing, regardless of how many years earlier it may have been or how much God has forgiven and used us since, we choose to hide them. The problem is that when things hide in darkness, it becomes the proverbial pea under the stack of mattresses.

Remember, darkness is where Satan dwells; he, like God, is no respecter of persons either. So, he doesn't care who he exposes, hurts, shames, or destroys! (John 10:10a). For many people in the Body of Christ, they walk around with what feels like a large millstone around their necks and feel as if at any moment they will fall into the lake of doom.

Years ago I knew a crack addict who was trying to get free from not only his addiction but from the lifestyle that kept him bound to those addictions. This man was the meanest-looking person I have ever met and had the size to back up any challenge that might come his way. After I worked with him for a little while, he really began to love and trust me.

One day he confessed to me a double murder he had committed years earlier. To support his lifestyle and habit, this guy formerly broke into crack houses and robbed them. Now, you have to be pretty mean and a bit crazy to do that sort of thing. One day, in a robbery gone wrong, guns were pulled and shots were fired. My friend was the only one left standing when the smoke finally settled.

I actually remembered the television news reports from years earlier when this all took place. For all those years, this man had to hide what he did in darkness. Even though he had experienced Christ and had changed in dramatic ways, he still could never walk down any street in peace. There was always the chance he would be discovered either by the police or by other crack dealers. So, with secret in hand, he was walking through life in constant shame, guilt, and fear of being exposed. He certainly was without any peace.

For the little girl mentioned above, she perhaps fell into the trap of seeking "love and acceptance" through multiple relationships. She sold her soul, as it were, for a bit of peace. Of course, it could never work. All these encounters served to do were to heap more and more guilt and shame on her life.

Imagine that years later, she comes to Christ and marries a godly young man. They have several wonderful children. She becomes one of the most committed saints in her church and a joy not only to the pastor but an example to so many others. Even though this thing she holds in darkness happened years earlier and even though she deeply repented and was forgiven by God, what would people think if they knew? So, darkness becomes her only means of self-preservation, or so she thinks.

For me, how could I ever let anyone know that my motives for being nice and loving were for my own self-centered benefit? What would people think if they knew that I so needed the approval of women that I would possibly compromise my own convictions and perhaps integrity for such? What would my wife think?

So, I made many unwise decisions—even going against the wisdom of my board and even my wife at times. If they really knew what was going on inside, what would they think of this mighty man of God? So, I had to disguise decisions as being either directives from God or my having a spiritual insight that they did not. Be careful when every other word out of your mouth is "God told me." Yes, God speaks today, but many people use this excuse far too often as a means of having things their way.

Demonic

Well, we have come just about full circle now in our "**Cycle of Pain.**" We started with the "**wound/love deficit**" in our life, which leads us to "**negative thinking**" about ourselves. We learned that at this point it will almost always lead us to "**sin**" or looking for love in all the wrong places. When we do sin at this point it will force us into "**darkness**" or having to hide or mask those things that our quest for love has taken us.

Now we come to the inevitable results of all of this and the place where darkness will always lead us; that is to the "**demonic.**" Let me make it clear to you at this point that in my opinion, a Born-Again, Spirit-Filled Christian cannot be demon-possessed. That is not what I am implying using the word in our cycle. What I am saying, however, is that we will be tormented!

When I go to Korea to minister I always willingly and joyfully submit to the Korean cultural traditions. When I go to a restaurant, for example, where the term *chair* seems to be nonexistent, I sit on the floor along with everyone else. With legs crossed and many prayers being offered that the blood will once again flow when I finally do get up, I happily eat.

In Korea very seldom will I ever use a fork when I am at a meal. Though at first it was offered, Rose and I made it our goal to become proficient with the chopsticks. At first, we considered using chopsticks a mandatory step to keep us from starvation; it worked. Soon, to the amazement of many of our dinner guests, we could pick up even the smallest of items handily.

And finally, regardless of whose home we enter, just like everyone else, I take my shoes off and at times replace them with a pair of prepared slippers. Even at churches in which I have preached, before I step up on the platform, the shoes come off and in most cases slippers go on. Now I say mostly because while my greatest intention is to follow Korean tradition, my feet have thus far rebelled and refuse to fit into slippers half their size! (LOL)

My point in these examples is simply that when I am in Korea or any places I may go, I am bound to follow the cultural customs before me. It is just like when I visit your home; I do not move furniture or rearrange drawers in the kitchen. That is your home and I am the guest; as such, I submit to the rules and dictates of your home. If I don't like the rules, I can leave!

The same is true when we dwell in darkness. Since darkness is where Satan lives, when we hang out in his domain, we are in many ways giving him authority over our lives. The only way to stop this is to leave the house. If you don't believe me, try going into someone's home and demanding in the Name of Jesus that they stop watching that television station.

Give it a shot and rebuke them for wearing those clothes or for using those words that you don't like. See how it works for you by having an open Bible in hand, shouting at the top of your lungs, "come out", trying to make them stop doing what you dislike. Regardless of all the slobber that may fly from our mouths or the religious terms we have dutifully memorized and now quote, when you are in someone else's home, the only way to stop what you don't like is to leave!

One of the tactics Satan loves the most is to torment us. He loves to subtly lead us down a path of destruction. When we reach the end and the inevitable happens, he loves to point out our faults and mockingly condemn us. A recent situation that stunned the world demonstrates this better than I ever could. I use this example with fear and trembling—not to judge or condemn but only to instruct.

A few years ago, Ted Haggard, a well-known pastor, leader, and champion for the Lord, was exposed in some sins. The affect of his sin affected thousands upon thousands and left many stunned in disbelief. For me it just further confirmed that, but for the grace of God, there went I. I realized that for all of us, with armor lowered and defenses down, we could be in the same position.

Brother Haggard was well known not only as the senior pastor of a large mega church but also as the head of a large Christian organization that served as watchmen on the wall for righteousness. One of the major platforms of this organization was to bring to light and fight the overly ambitious agenda of the homosexual community, which, this organization believed, was designed to force its beliefs into mainstream America.

I can just imagine how every time this man of God stood in the pulpit or spoke on this subject at national events, some well-informed demon was whispering in his ear things such as, "You hypocrite!" Perhaps Ted heard the jeers of the devil mocking him every time he presented the biblical admonition on the topic. I would think that every time he looked at his wife and children, an arrow would have pierced his heart and conscience. The Tormentor is always at work *"to steal and kill and destroy"* (John 10:10a).

You see, when we live in and hold things in darkness, we give license to the Enemy; he takes full advantage of it by tormenting us. He catches us in every hypocritical slip and makes sure we don't forget what we've done or are yet doing. Again, I am in no way judging or making light of the events in Ted Haggard's life but merely am using this all-too-well-known example to demonstrate the devil's tactics. My heart grieves over what has happened to this man of God. Although I have not gone down the exact path he did, I have made my own paths in life that have at times drawn similar words of torment from the Evil One. I have heard his whispers in my ears as he makes one accusation after another while he jeers every time. Have you?

For the little girl, now grown up, every time she teaches her students in Sunday school on the purity Christ desires from our lives, she hears those whispers from her tormentor. Should she learn of one of her students being involved in a promiscuous life style, she couldn't help but see the reruns of her past as it is played through her mind. And God forbid, if one day one of her own children should choose a similar path as she did, the weight of the torment may seem unbearable.

For me, as I said earlier, I know what I am talking about here. I have at times rehearsed over and over again mistakes, poor judgment calls, and whatever else the results of my wounding may have caused me or my loved ones. I have by now learned the tactic and torment of the Enemy. Normally, those tormenting accusations are at their loudest when we are doing something great for God!

The **"demonic"**, unfortunately, is not the end of the cycle. It is just that—a cycle—and as such, just continues around and around. There will be new wounds followed by refreshed or new negative thoughts that will be followed by sin trying to disprove these thoughts and then darkness and more of the demonic. Over and over it goes.

Chapter 12

Breaking the Cycle

L ike I said earlier, I have been teaching on "the Cycle of Pain"
      wherever I go. The cycle seems to have a tremendous impact
      in that it gives people the ability to actually see with their
own eyes what has been happening to them. It explains to them the
on-again, off-again relationship many have had with the Lord as well
as with their own continual struggle with sin.

While I was teaching this one time, I think Rose was listening
more to the Lord than to me. The results were what she calls "the Cycle
of Healing". Using the same model of the cycle I had drawn up on the
board, she showed a simple approach to breaking the cycle in our lives.
It is from this teaching that I share the following.

I have discovered that many of the things of the Lord are far sim-
pler to follow and to grasp than we often make them. Consider the
Ten Commandments, for example. God gave Moses 10 rules, not sug-
gestions, for us to follow. By the time of Jesus, estimates are that the
Bible's list of instructions for us grew to well over 600. Listen to how
simple Jesus made it.

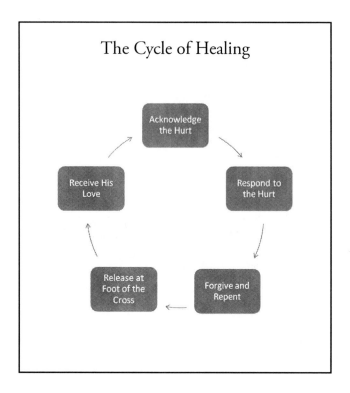

".. . Love the Lord your God with all your heart and with all your soul and with all your mind. This is the first and greatest commandment. And the second is like it: Love your neighbor as yourself. All the Law and the Prophets hang on these two commandments" (Mt. 22:37-40).

You see, in all of our great wisdom we believe, for some reason, that we need to improve on what God says and does. When will we learn that attempts at improvement always seem to get us into trouble? Apparently this is a lesson God hopes we soon learn, as He felt it necessary to repeat it twice in the Book of Proverbs. *"There is a way that seems right to a man, but in the end it leads to death"* (Prov. 14:12 and 16:25).

If those two verses don't shake us back to reality where realizing that God knows best is concerned, then perhaps the following from Isaiah will do the trick. By the way, I suppose that the television series, "Father Knows Best!", from back in the '50s or '60s had a biblical truth in its title. Anyway, listen to Isaiah's simple yet profound statement from the heart of God.

"For my thoughts are not your thoughts, neither are your ways my ways, declares the Lord. As the heavens are higher than the earth, so are my ways higher than your ways and my thoughts than your thoughts" (Isa. 55:8-9.)

Acknowledge the Hurt

As simple as it might sound at this point, the first thing we need to do to be healed and to be set free from our wounds is to simply acknowledge or admit we have a problem. We like to say it this way, "You need to hurt enough to want help." Until we can say "ouch", why would we ever pay attention to a sensitive spot on our body?

In truth, we would have never accepted the atoning sacrifice of Jesus' death for our sins unless we really thought we needed it. I mean, why would we need someone to save us unless we really believed we needed to be saved? When the Spirit of God convicted us that ***"There is no one righteous, not even one . . . for all have sinned and fall short of the glory of God"*** (John 3:10, 23), we quickly understood that something was really wrong and that we needed a Savior.

In our effort to carry ourselves as mature, Bible-believing, faith-filled Christians, at times we have been told that it was wrong to acknowledge pain or discomfort. I say, if it is broken, admit it and see if there is anything we can do to fix it. Only when we get to the point of saying, "My life is miserable and I am sick and tired of being sick and tired", can we begin to do what it takes for healing in this area. On any journey in life there is a starting point. I believe this is the one necessary for healing.

It seems as if the higher we climb up the spiritual ladder, if there is such a thing, the harder it is to admit we have problems. Having taught at seven pastors' conferences in Korea in the last five years and after having spoken individually to more than 300 to 400 pastors and their wives, this point became clearer to me.

For whatever reasons, most Korean pastors cannot show their emotions outside of the pulpit—at least not when they are feeling bad. It seems like these dear saints just grin and bear it. It really is heartbreaking to watch, but unfortunately we see this same pattern in so many people. The brokenness seen in what I consider to be some of the dearest and most spiritual people in the world will bring you to tears. I suspect, however, that it is the same for pastors universally. It was for me.

Whoever you are reading this chapter today, please, for your own sake and that of your family and friends, finally be honest and admit you are miserable. It is OK to hurt. Doing so is not a sign of weakness but is a sign of your own humanness. Acknowledging that those we are supposed to honor actually brought some real hurt to our lives is not disrespect but is the first step to healing.

Respond to the Hurt

When our sons were younger, we had many different kinds of pets and animals around the house and yard. We always seemed to have some adventure going on. At one point we raised rats and mice for the purpose of selling them to pet stores and other individuals who might need these tasty morsels for their reptiles. My wife had one phrase for that and it was . . . *ewwwww.*

One day I was in the back yard trying to catch a few of the escapees that had run under our shed. On the ground next to the shed were some 4 x 4 blocks of hollow glass that were used in some homes to bring daylight into the bathroom without violating privacy. Not thinking, while I wore shorts, I knelt down on these blocks and stretched under the shed to catch some of the varmints.

The first two or three retrievals went fine, but then the inevitable happened. The blocks gave way under my weight; my knee went right through them. It didn't take long to admit I was hurt, so I responded quickly by shouting for my wife. At the moment I had two choices. I could lie on the ground and bleed to death, or I could go for help at the hospital. Realizing that this was way beyond my expertise with a bandage or my typical macho response of, "Oh, it will be OK; I can handle it", we went to the hospital, where I received 22 stitches.

Perhaps it is no coincidence that you are reading this book right now. Maybe, just maybe, it has been set before you as a means of responding to the hurts you have carried for so long. Maybe you were recently talking to a friend who was telling you about some church or program that they attended and how it made such a difference in that person's heart and life.

All I know, beloved, is that to get the help you need, you have to respond—the sooner, the better. Until you take the first steps in this journey, there will likely be no relief; you'll experience more and more worry, hurt, and discouragement in your life. Simply put, the more you delay, the more you pay!

Forgive and Repent

That day many years ago when the Lord spoke to me and told me that I needed to deal with all of the anger and bitterness I was harboring toward my mom, I really knew— for the first time perhaps—I had to forgive her. When the pain coming from the hurts people have inflicted on us is so severe, a simple religious, "I forgive my mom in Jesus' Name" won't do the job.

Why, you might ask? Because the reality of our experience at that moment is likely more of a surface confession and does not take into account the depth of our wounds. It is like years ago when I asked my oldest son to forgive me and he responded quickly that he did and that he loved me. I knew then that it was the 20-something-year-old Marine talking to me, but that the little boy inside had no clue. We must forgive from the heart! (Mt. 18:35).

A quick search on the Internet will reveal that so many groups, both secular and Christian, are beginning to realize the necessity of forgiveness. We know that unforgiveness and bitterness are the breeding grounds for many diseases. It is possible to be so bitter that you never get better unless you make some radical changes in your heart.

Over the years I have heard many stories and testimonies about the wonderful power of restoration that took place after someone forgave. None is perhaps as dramatic and instantaneous as the one that years ago I read about in one of Dr. Yonggie Cho's books.

He told about a woman in his church that had come for prayer several times for healing of a partially paralyzed face. Having seen so many miracles before in his life and ministry in the past, he was somewhat shocked and frustrated that after so many attempts at prayer, this poor woman was still not healed. In this particular session in his office, as he expressed his frustration to the Lord, the Lord spoke to him.

The Lord told Dr. Cho to ask this woman if she had anyone in her life that she could not forgive. She immediately responded in the affirmative and began telling him why she could not forgive her mother-in-law. She told Dr. Cho that she just could not forgive this woman. So he asked her if she could at least pray in faith and ask the Lord to do for her what she herself could not do.

She said she would try and began to pray something like this: "Dear Father, I cannot forgive my mother-in-law for what she has done to me, but you said that I had to forgive. I am asking you to help me by forgiving her through me." Dr. Cho said that immediately, as she said those words, her face became normal and the paralysis was gone. It so shocked both the woman and Dr. Cho that he said he immediately began telling God that he forgave this deacon and that elder, etc. (LOL)

I cannot promise you that your healing and deliverance will be as dramatic. Mine wasn't at all, but one thing I do know and have experienced is that forgiveness sets us free. It seems as if so many people have their own take on how to forgive, when to forgive, and what that other person may need to do before we forgive, but being the simple-minded person I am, I will just go to the Scriptures and let them talk for themselves.

Let's have a look in Matthew 18 and let the Word of God speak for itself. Since this is such an important subject, I hope you don't mind if I share the story in its entirety. Pray for an open mind and a willing heart and, if necessary, for God's help to forgive through you.

Then Peter came to Jesus and asked, "Lord, how many times shall I forgive my brother when he sins against me? Up to seven times?" Jesus answered, "I tell you, not seven times, but seventy-seven times.

Therefore, the kingdom of heaven is like a king who wanted to settle accounts with his servants. As he began the settlement, a man who owed him ten thousand talents was brought to him. Since he was not able to pay, the master ordered that he and his wife and his children and all that he had be sold to repay the debt.

The servant fell on his knees before him, 'Be patient with me,' he begged, 'and I will pay back everything.' The servant's master took pity on him, cancelled the debt and let him go.

But when that servant went out, he found one of his fellow servants who owed him a hundred denarii. He grabbed him and began to choke him. 'Pay back what you owe me!' he demanded. His fellow servant fell to his knees and begged him. 'Be patient with me, and I will pay you back.'

*But he refused. Instead, he went off and had the man
thrown into prison until he could pay the debt.
When the other servants saw what had happened,
they were greatly distressed and went and told
their master everything that had happened.*

*Then the master called the servant in. 'You wicked ser-
vant,' he said, 'I cancelled all that debt of yours because
you begged me to. Shouldn't you have had mercy on your
fellow servant just as I had on you?' In anger his master
turned him over to the jailers to be tortured, until he
should pay back all he owed.*

*This is how my heavenly Father will treat each of you
unless you forgive your brother from your heart"*
(Mt. 18:21-35).

No matter what your current view on forgiveness is, I think we
can all agree that it is extremely important that we do so, at least for
the sake of being obedient to the Word of God (Mt. 6:14, 15). But, it
is also important for the sake of our own well-being. Would you agree?
Obedience to the words of Jesus should be our greatest desire.

When I read these verses, I do not hear a do-or-die ultimatum,
but I am hearing a "do this for your own spiritual, emotional and physical health." However, I don't know why we are sometimes so afraid to
link a holy, loving Father with some strong language towards His children. Make the call for yourself as to whether you believe this is a command from Jesus, but as for me and my house, we choose to forgive,
having experienced the wonderful release of doing so!

I think that in this story the analogy is pretty clear. The King is
the Lord; the servants can represent any one of us. Servant number
one is called in to account for his debt and can't pay. His judgment is
basically to pay for a debt for which he could never pay; thus an eternal

sentence of doom is his lot. Servant number two owes servant one a mere pittance compared to the debt he, himself, was forgiven.

Instead of forgiving his fellow servant/brother, he tries to issue the same punishment the King first offered him. You can be sure that regardless of how severe we have been hurt and offended by others, we have no right to try to sentence them to eternal punishment. When the other servants hear of this harsh and clearly unfair treatment, it's off to the King they go to complain.

When he hears about it, he is furious—as you might imagine—and throws servant number one back to jail to pay his unpayable debt. Now no matter how you look at this story Jesus is sharing here, it didn't turn out well for the first guy, to be sure!

Can I suggest here that when you and I refuse to release someone from whatever sins they have committed against us, things work out far worse for us than they were in the first place? Is that a fair assumption? If so, based on that alone, why would we not want to forgive someone? When we know in advance that whatever pain and suffering the offense may have caused us may get worse if we don't forgive, who in their right mind wouldn't?

I am not at all trying to minimize some of the horrendous things some people have had done to them in their lives or to write them off as some minor offense that simply needs to be overlooked. No, I am simply saying that the end does not justify the means if you really think about it. Besides, going back to Dr. Cho's experience with the woman in his office, I believe God will help us to do whatever it takes for freedom and release!

I want to say one more thing on the subject before we move on. Several years ago, after a service in which my wife taught on forgiveness, one woman approached one of the leaders and was furious. She felt my wife's message was not only off base but also was insensitive. This woman shared with the leader the hideous things someone had done to her in the past and how my wife had some nerve to suggest that she had to forgive the person who had done these things to her.

Unfortunately, this leader felt that just coming out and telling people they had to forgive without knowing what they had actually gone through was insensitive. He actually defended this woman and felt my wife's teaching was wrong to impose such pressure to the much-wounded woman. It seemed that to do so was to impose more grief on this poor soul.

In an effort to be gentle, yet knowing in advance it will sound insensitive, let me say this: Jesus Himself said we must forgive. End of story! Now, if He says that we must, then I am going to assume that by His Spirit He will help to accomplish the task. In other words, we do not have to fight this struggle alone, but we have the assurance that Someone much bigger than us will help us! The imperative to forgive is not predicated on the severity of the action committed against us!

Release at the Foot of the Cross

The Old Testament picture of the laver (Basin), seen first in Exodus 30:17-21, to me has always been a wonderful image during certain times of prayer. This was a piece of furniture placed in the Tabernacle in the Wilderness that Moses had built according to God's design. It was basically a basin for the washing and purification of Aaron and his sons before they entered the Tent of Meeting, lest they die.

Made from the mirrors (since glass was not around at this time, these mirrors would have most likely been made of carefully polished brass) of the devoted women who served at the entrance to the Tent of Meeting (Ex. 38:8), this piece of furniture would reflect your image when you looked at it. Because of the manner in which it would have been made, likely beaten into form by a mallet of some sort, the image would have been distorted.

As the priests would turn the lever for the water to come out as they washed their hands and feet, they would obviously be staring at their image, reflected by the brass, at the same time. So, this became then a mirror to reflect and a fountain to cleanse. The analogy could be this: As we look into the Word of God and see our poor reflection, distorted as it were from that which God would have it, we wash with the washing of water through the Word (Eph. 5:26). In short, this was a place of repentance for which the priests stopped daily.

When I am praying and meditating on the symbolism here, I get a picture of my coming before the foot of the cross and laying before it all my dirty laundry. Here I leave all my hurts and wounds and unforgiveness and bitterness, along with any negative thoughts or thoughts of retaliation. I make a determined effort to lay down anything and everything that may keep me from experiencing intimacy with my Father.

So, as someone in the freezing weather would be covered with many layers of clothing to keep warm, the closer I get to the fire, one by one each negative feeling and emotion goes. Off with the masks I have been wearing—those things that I have worn to disguise my true heart—in the Name of Jesus. Next, I strip away the shame and then the guilt I have been wearing in association with these issues. I then reach for the desires to harm myself because of what I have been experiencing and lay it down as well.

As each layer is removed, it seems to get a bit more difficult as I fear that the Fire I stand before won't understand me or will not take this chill out of my heart. But in faith I reach for the next few layers meant to protect my tender heart; off come the anger, resentment, and bitterness. The closer I get to the main issue, I realize that I am getting closer and closer to standing here naked before the cross of the One who gave His life for me that I might live.

Now, sensing His gaze upon my heart and feeling His hurt over the hurt I am feeling, I am more determined than ever to get closer and to remove all that hinders. Finally, I am left standing before Him with nothing left but that person who brought so much pain and sorrow to my life for all these years. So in final desperation, I cry, "Here, I lay him/her also before you!"

As before this wonderful Cross I stand, stripped of all the things that were weighing me down, I ask for the cleansing and washing of His Precious Blood. *In fact, the law requires that nearly everything be cleansed with blood, and without the shedding of blood there is no forgiveness* (Heb. 9:22).

Asking for the appropriation of His Precious Blood to cleanse me and free me from the weight I can no longer carry, I begin to feel a peace I have never known (John 16:33), followed by a joy I cannot explain (Ps. 16:11; Acts 2:28).

Finally, somehow, I know that if I take my eyes off of Him, I may try to take back some of these things I have just laid before Him, so there is one more thing I must ask: "Jesus, would you place the cross between me and this person, so that from this point forward, if I should see or think about him or her again, I see this person through Your cross—that is, see this one as you do, with love?"

> *"Therefore, if you are offering your gift at the altar and there remember that your brother has something against you, leave your gift there in front of the altar. First go and be reconciled to your brother; then come and offer your gift"* (Mt. 5:23-24).

There are some things that we need to remember at this point. First, the fact that I may forgive and release someone does not mean that the person has to or is obligated to do the same toward me. You cannot make someone forgive, want to hang out with, or love you. That is between him or her and God alone. I do think, however, as I saw in my situation between me and my mom, the more you release someone from the anger and unforgiveness you have toward him or her, the more sensitive the individual's heart **might** get and the closer **you may** became.

We also need to understand that being reconciled with someone does not have to always happen face to face. Circumstances may prove this impossible. There are many scenarios where this may be the case, but for easy understanding, think about the need to be reconciled with someone who has long been dead.

In the case of someone who is deceased or in circumstances making a face-to-face meeting impossible, I believe reconciliation can happen here at the cross. The main point again is laying these things down so that we might be free from the layers of hurt and pain that may hinder our feeling His loving arms around us!

I have to be honest with you here and say that there have been some people that I have had to bring before the cross many times. Because of the intensity of whatever I was feeling about them and the severity of the perceived or real hurt I felt they caused, it has taken several trips down this road. Let me assure you that you will never hear the Lord say, "*Come on; not again!*"

Keep in mind that it is the greatest desire of the Father to hold you in tender intimacy. He is the one that provided the cross for the sake of all of our sins so that He could once again share in and experience the fellowship He had had with man in the Garden.

> *The man and his wife heard the sound of the Lord God as*
> *he was walking in the garden in the cool of the day, and*
> *they hid from the Lord God among the trees of the garden.*
> *But the Lord God called to the man, "Where are you?"*
> (Gen. 3:8-9).

This particular day would have been far different than previous days. Before the man and his wife sinned, when they heard the Lord God walking in the garden, they would have run with all their might to see Him and to be with Him. Long, early morning walks would have turned into late-evening strolls as God and His greatest joy—humanity—would have been just enjoying one another. No time restraints, no agenda, no worries—just pure, unhindered, intimate fellowship.

I don't know about you, but at this moment, nothing seems worth my missing out on one of these strolls with my Papa. There is so much

I want to know about Him. I know that in that place of intimacy with Him, nothing else in the world would matter. I would feel at complete, unexplainable peace. I would experience unbelievable joy and happiness.

To be honest, somehow I think He would, too!

Receive His Love

I remember learning years ago that there were basically two different ways most people learned things. One way would be by sight. In other words, they could read and comprehend. Then this would place the memory of that information somewhere in the brain; it could be used for recall whenever necessary.

Another way some people learn is by hearing the information. For whatever reason, they have a greater chance of absorbing what they hear than what they see. Either way, learning is learning, but the challenge, all too often, is getting these lessons from the head to the heart. As I stated earlier in this book, I had the head knowledge of God's love but not the experiential knowledge.

In other words, I knew the truth, but because the truth for whatever reason wasn't penetrating my heart, this truth didn't set me free. **So, the battle within me was that I knew something was supposed to be a certain way, but my experience was so vastly different that it seemed to thrust me into unbelief.** For me, and I am sure for many of you, this difference between truth and reality can be devastating.

Knowing that many of us would have experiences in our lives, regardless of how real or perceived they might be, that would be contrary to the truth of God's Word, the author of Romans gives this admonition. *Let God be true, and every man a liar* (Rom 3:4).

One of the reasons we as the Body of Christ, in my opinion, have become so impotent is because we have watered down the power and impact of God's Word by diluting it with personal experience. We have become very good at believing that our experiences, rather than the

Word, ultimately represent truth. When this happens to a person or, for that matter, to any society, what follows can only be disastrous.

As one who has been a Christian now for over 35 years, having been in various "levels" of leadership for most of that time, can I take some liberty as a senior member of the Body of Christ? Can I speak to you as one who has experienced far more of what I am speaking about here than I would like to think? May I say it bluntly without feeling the pressure of being "politically correct" or being afraid I might step on some dear saints' toes?

The fact is, there are times we need our toes stepped on so that we can take our heads out of the clouds and look down again in humility to see what our problems are. To quote my mom, if I might, "Hey, you are getting too big for your britches!" What makes us think that after 20, 35, or even 50 years as Christians that we are beyond correcting or in need of a good dose of humility?

> *Your attitude should be the same as that of Christ Jesus;*
> *Who being in very nature God, did not consider equality*
> *with God something to be grasped, but made himself noth-*
> *ing, taking the very nature of a servant, being made in*
> *human likeness. And being found in appearance as a man,*
> *he humbled himself and became obedient to death—even*
> *death on a cross! Therefore God exalted him . . .*
> (Phil. 2:5-9a).

How dare we think we can take the Breath of God, breathe it in ourselves, and let what comes out be defined as His Breath alone? *All Scripture is God breathed and is useful for teaching, rebuking, correcting and training in righteousness, so that the man of God may be thoroughly equipped for every good work* (2 Tim. 3:16-17).

Forgive me for ranting about this, but I have become so tired of myself and many others who at times have said or lived things in arrogance, calling them "truth", and who as a result have hindered so many from coming into the kingdom. At this point, I think the world is tired of our empty words, clear hypocrisy, and the mishandling of the Great Treasure with which we have been entrusted and for which they so desperately need and long.

OK, I'm done. It is at this point my wife would at times need to remind me that I am supposed to be "Mr. Father's Love" and that it is time to show it. Lest I go off on another tangent, I will leave it right there! (LOL)

I think the Word of God is the obvious place to go for a clear understanding of God's love for us. To receive and believe, we need to see or hear something worth believing. In the next chapter I want to share several verses that I believe will, if you look at, listen to, and meditate on them, help you to get things from your head to your heart.

After each verse I will share a few thoughts pertaining to that particular verse. Basically, these will be some of the things the Father has shown Rose and me concerning His love as reflected in the verse. Keep in mind that these are personal snippets from us and that the most important part is the verse itself and how Daddy speaks to you through it!

Chapter 13

Verses to Meditate On

1. ". . . I have loved you with an everlasting love; I have drawn you with loving-kindness" (Jer. 31:3).

When using the word *revelation* to describe our coming to realize and understand God's love, as I mentioned earlier in this book, it is important to know what a *revelation* is. Simply put, when you pull back a curtain, what you see on the other side, is something that has been there the whole time. It has only been hidden by the curtain. A revelation is the pulling back of a curtain, enabling us to see something of God that has always been.

The verse above is clear that God has "always" loved us. His love is *"everlasting,"* meaning that it will not end. But when did this love start? Again, we only need to look at John 3:16 to know that He loved us before He formed us. This should give us pause. The fact is that Papa loved us "before" we ever had a chance to sin, make a mistake, or fail. Knowing this would be the case in all of our lives, He sent Jesus to forgive those sins and to provide a way for us to enter into fellowship with Him.

Not only that, but the truth is that you and I did nothing to warrant, earn, or deserve this love. He drew us to Himself just because He wanted to. That has to mean that every human being that was ever conceived was someone that the Spirit of God desired to draw to the heart of the Father, through Christ. Just because so many people may reject His drawing does not mean it didn't or isn't still happening.

And, the fact that we were drawn with "*loving-kindness*" tells me that He, the Almighty, our Daddy, is someone that we can come near to and know intimately. It reflects His willingness and desire to walk in fellowship and partnership with each of us. In fact, Revelation 3:20 says that Jesus is knocking at the door of our hearts in hopes that we will open up so He can have fellowship with us!

You, my friend, have been drawn when you didn't even know it. The love He has for you will never end. The next time some devil tries to convince you otherwise, refer him to the verse above, but more importantly, believe it yourself.

2. "*Before I formed you in the womb I knew you, before you were born I set you apart; I appointed you as a prophet to the nations*" (Jer. 1:5).

Before we even get sidetracked thinking that this verse only applies to the man to whom it was written, let us remember what Peter said at the home of Cornelius, the Roman centurion, when the Holy Spirit led him to share the Gospel with these Gentiles. **"... I now realize how true it is that God does not show favoritism"** (Acts 10:34).

God knew you and me before we were ever thought of by our parents. In His overall plan for the ages and *regardless* of the circumstances leading up to your and my conception, the Father planned for and had a plan for us. Perhaps it wasn't to be a prophet like Jeremiah, but there is and always has been a tremendous, impacting destiny outlined for you. That makes you and me an intricate part of God's plan and purpose for this world and for eternity (Eph. 2:10).

At best, while on this earth, we are spokesmen (Ambassadors) for Him and His love. We fulfill this tall order by the living of a life that has been impacted by this love. To the extent that you and I know and experience His love and affections, we will be mirrors reflecting this love to the world. I didn't say we would impact people necessarily by our **knowledge** of this love, but I know we will once it becomes our **experience**.

The verse above also tells me something else that is so very important for all of us, from time to time, to hear. It is: we are not a mistake! Again, regardless of the circumstances behind our conception, in God's eyes we are not a mistake, misfortune, or misfit. Now, wrapped in His arms of love, we can ask Him to reveal His purposes for our being. One of His purposes is, without question, that we rest in those arms.

3. How great is the love (agape) the Father has lavished on us, that we should be called children of God! And that is what we are . . . (1 John 3:1).

I sense here the excitement and genuine sincerity from one who himself has tasted of the matchless love flowing from the Father. Regardless of the hardships or struggles John may have been enduring at the time, he still cannot contain himself when he thinks of the intimate relationship he has had, is experiencing now, and will yet enjoy with the Father and one he hopes you and I would also embrace.

First, he mentions this unbelievable love that is *lavished* on us from the heart of God. When I hear this word *lavish,* I cannot help but think of a super-abundant, overflowing, non-stop love that only He who Himself is love could produce. Not only does His love exceed anything we could have ever imagined or experienced from mother or father, husband or wife, or anyone else for that matter, it is unconditional and never-ending as well.

Then, there seems to be this emphasis on our being *children* of God. Where we will lose the effect of this right here is when we try to relate our childhood experiences to what John is referring to. Let me be perfectly clear here and say that there is no comparison! What you and I may have experienced as far as being a child of our parents is concerned, regardless of how good it may have been, still falls far short of what it means to be a child of God.

The truth is that our Heavenly Father never makes mistakes, has the purest of motives, is not intimidated or embarrassed when we make mistakes, and is the epitome of all that patience is. Papa forgives and forgets, never leaves nor forsakes, is not distracted by "life", and has already proven His willingness to die for us.

Being a child of God takes us to a level that is unattainable through anyone else, anywhere, ever. His door is always open, His heart always engaged, and His love, as we have already seen, is being *lavished* upon us. And as if to further emphasize what he is telling us concerning our being children of God, John again affirms that **that is what we are.**

Apparently, when one meditates on the wonders of God and all He has done and will yet do in us, for us, and through us, our hearts and minds cannot help but be overwhelmed. When David meditated on the love of God and how important and special he was to the Holy One, his heart burst forth with the words in the this next Scripture.

4. For you created my inmost being; you knit me together in my mother's womb. I praise you because I am fearfully and wonderfully made; your works are wonderful, I know that full well. My frame was not hidden from you when I was made in the secret place. When I was woven together in the depths of the earth, your eyes saw my unformed body. All the days ordained for me were written in your book before one of them came to be. How precious to me are your thoughts Oh God! How vast is the sum of them! Were I to count them, they would outnumber the grains of sand. When I awake, I am still with you (Ps. 139:13-18).

It is impossible to really think about our conception and birth without really understanding how valued and special we are. Frankly, I think the enemy knew this and through the horrid sin of abortion has been on an all-out assault to minimize our thoughts about conception and birth. The killing of more than 50 million children in the United States alone over the last 30-plus years has, for so many, removed the mystery, amazement, and frankly, the respect for life!

Let me be very quick before I go any further in this discussion by saying this to those of you who may have had an abortion or been an agreeable party to one. When we repent—that is, recognize our sin as sin and ask Him to forgive us—God forgives, restores, and even forgets. If you are feeling any guilt or shame right now because of these things, it is not coming from Him but is perhaps one of the inevitable results or consequence of such things.

Stop reading right now and just get quiet before your Daddy. Allow Him to hold you, warm your soul, and whisper into your heart how much He loves and adores you. I believe He wants to pour grace on your grief, love on your loss, and bring peace to your pain. Our God is such an amazing God!

Now if you can remember back to the Health 101 class back in your school days, you will remember the simple fact about the beginning of life. We learned that it took one "egg" from the mother and one "sperm" from the father, joining together, to form a baby. While this may sound very simple, I think we have lost the depth of what really happens here.

Consider this. A doctor once told me that for that "one sperm" to actually make it to the "one egg", it would be accompanied by anywhere from 20 million to as many as 100 million other sperm. Now stop and think about that for a minute. How can you be a mistake? How could your birth have been "by chance"? You are not only "one in a million" but one in 20 million or possibly 100 million!

That, my friend, ought to cause us to pause for at least several moments as we ponder the preciseness of our God in allowing us to be born. The moment we were conceived, long before our parents would have had any idea we were there, God did. And, as David suggests, He was not only overwhelmed and excited, but He stayed with us and formed us into the precious son or daughter He wanted us to be. He was knitting within us everything we would need to fulfill the tremendous destiny He had for us.

Let me say it again: you could not have been a mistake regardless of the circumstances that led up to your birth or regardless of what anyone says. You have been created and designed with purpose and destiny. And when David says, ***How precious to me are your thoughts, O God!*** (Ps. 139:17), he is talking about God's thoughts about him . . . about His thoughts towards you and me.

Let me try and give you a visual on this. Go to any beach on the planet and scoop up a bucket full of sand in one of those toy buckets our kids or grandkids have. Now, let's just say that each individual grain of sand in your bucket represents a thought you have had about God in the course of your lifetime. Those are a lot of thoughts, aren't they?

Now, while you are standing there on that beach with your bucket in your hands, look around at all of the sand that is still left on the beach. If you could count each grain of sand left on the beach, it still would not fully represent all of the thoughts that Papa has for you. David seems to indicate that if you tried to count all of the thoughts God had for you, you would fall asleep counting. When you woke up, His thoughts of love and affirmation toward you would still be headed in your direction!

If there ever were ever a time to stop and shout "Hallelujah", it would be right now. No wonder the 24 elders in Revelation 4:9-11 laid down their crowns before the Throne of God and proclaimed, ***"You are worthy, our Lord and God, to receive glory and honor and power, for you created all things, and by your will they were created and have their being."***

When Rose was pregnant with our first son, Vince, she wanted to make something special for him. She went to the fabric store and carefully picked out some yarn—the exact color and quality that best represented the love she felt in her heart for him. She spent many hours filled with anticipation, joy, and expectation as she knit together what became a beautiful little outfit for our son. Words cannot describe what she felt with every stitch as she looked forward to our first son.

That, my friend, is again a small picture of what our Father saw and felt in His heart toward you and me. Every "stitch" in our being was carefully woven together to make what His heart was feeling toward us. Although Papa is not restricted or controlled by time, if He did have a calendar, He would have crossed off each day as He waited with great anticipation, joy, and expectation to hear your voice. Again, HALLELUJAH!

5. *"From one man he made every nation of men, that they should inhabit the whole earth; and he determined the times set for them and the exact places where they should live. God did this so that men would seek him and perhaps reach out for him and find him, though he is not far from each one of us"* (Acts 17:26-27).

I love to watch Westerns and Medieval/Gladiator type of movies. Of course, they are always more exciting to watch when I am eating meat and sitting in my "man chair". (LOL) I am not sure of all the psychology behind my attraction to these two periods in history, but I can tell you that I have often at times daydreamed about what it would have been like to live in one of these two eras—that is until I really began to understand what the verses above were saying.

The Father knew exactly where and when we would be born; He planned this with purpose. How many times have you thought or said something like, "If I had only been born 100 years ago" or "I was born 100 years too late"? The fact is that if you were, or if I had been born in one of those two eras that are represented in the movies I love to watch, we may never have met Jesus!

Can you imagine what we are reading here? God planned for you and me to be born, not only in the exact place (culture, country, or city) we were, but to the exact family. Whatever we may have experienced by being born in the "place" at which we were born or in the "family" we were born into, God has used every experience as a means for our seeking Him and His love and redemption. Again, we can see that there were no mistakes!

At first, I know this can bring up so many questions as to "why" we may have had to endure this or that, but let's not get sidetracked. The bottom line is that He knew everything and was working what the devil meant for evil into a course leading us to the good. (See Gen. 50:19-20 and Rom. 8:28).

Armed with this knowledge and understanding, it begins to free us to really live and enjoy the life the Father has laid before us. We now realize that we have value and purpose and that there is no one on earth who can keep us from what God has for us. Go forth, precious one, and enjoy the fruit and abundance before you in this new land of hope and promise.

6. He tends his flock like a shepherd; He gathers the lambs in his arms and carries them close to his heart; he gently leads those that have young (Isa. 40:11).

I am sure that by now you have either read or heard about some of the wonderful analogies from real-life shepherds as they compare what they do in contrast to the Bible's reference to the Great Shepherd—Jesus. The genuine care and concern by these people for their sheep is not only amazing but is a powerful pictorial as to how the Lord cares for and views us. Since He made both shepherd and sheep, we can understand His wisdom!

Let's get out of the way our first inclination, which is perhaps to compare real sheep with Christians as being "dumb animals". OK, we said it; now that should be enough about that. Another analogy between man and beast here would be how a sheep, if somehow rolled over on its back (being "cast"), cannot get up by itself. This is often the case, as well, for a Christian who slips under the weight of sin and really needs a helping hand to get up and get going again.

The main impact the above verse has on me is how the Father, Son, and Holy Spirit combine to take care of us. He tends to our needs, draws us to Himself, and holds us near His heart. At the present time I have six grandchildren. My heart is flooded with warm memories of the times I have been with them and when they have allowed me to hold and comfort them. Each has his or her own special personality and responds differently during similar circumstances, but when they do reach out to my outstretched arms, it is one of the greatest feelings I have ever experienced in my life—second, of course, to when my own sons have done this in the past and occasionally still do.

I have already discussed the importance of touch and of our having safe hugs. Several times in the past few years I have been the recipient of such a hug from godly men and women who stood in as parents for me and who brought tremendous comfort and healing. These times have been priceless to me. I would suggest that all of us need those arms, those shoulders. and that heart in our lives. The Father stands more than willing to be all that we need.

Then, He says that *he gently leads those that have young.* What an amazing analogy and picture of our loving, caring Father. Think about those that have *young* with them and of all the possible things that could be going on in their hearts and lives. Needless to say, there would be so many concerns surrounding having little ones running around that it would be easy to be consumed or distracted.

Not only that, but there would be the obvious need to slow down and move at the pace of that child. I mean, after all, their legs are shorter and their schedules are nothing like ours. They cannot understand urgency; frankly, their attention span is limited, to say the least. So the parent is left to adjust to all of these needs in the life of his or her child.

So it is that our Daddy, laying aside—if necessary—the urgency of the moment, is careful in our lives to lead us, even when we do not realize we are being led. Knowing our tendency to get caught up in the cares of this world, He still has a way of leading us to the place of destiny He has for each of us. Simply put, our Father doesn't seem interested in dragging us kicking and screaming!

7. "The Lord your God is with you, he is mighty to save. He will take great delight in you, he will quiet you with his love, he will rejoice over you with singing" (Zeph. 3:17).

I can understand the Lord being with me and His being more than able to reach down and save me, but it always intrigues me to hear that He delights in me. I guess I could give you the "correct" definition of "*delight*" here, but I have come up with my own that suits me just fine. Just the word itself, coming from the lips of God in referring to how He feels about me, is amazing.

But for me, when I hear that my Daddy delights in me, I get the sense that He really likes me. Oh sure, He loves me—I get that, but to think that besides loving me, He really likes me, is too wonderful to grasp sometimes. I am reminded of some people that I really love, but if I'm honest, I don't really like to be around them too much. Surely you can think of a few examples of this in your own life as well.

There are however, many people I just really like to be around and spend time with. Regardless of whether or not we are doing much talking, just to be around some people, for me, is such a *delight*. Listening to them talk, relate, dream, or just "being themselves" makes my heart warm and in some ways makes me feel secure. What I am saying is that God really likes you. You are a *delight* to Him!

146

Often while I'm merely around some people, the concerns of life and the fears that seemed to be overwhelming to me are changed into feelings of peace and rest. Love has a way of covering and shielding us from so many of life's potentially destructive events. There is quietness in our souls when we really know that we are loved.

Finally, this verse says that our Father rejoices over us with singing. I want to relate to you an amazing experience my wife had with two of our grandchildren. We've had times in which the grandkids have spent the night at our home with us. When my oldest son's twins, Cole and Jade, first started to spend the night with us, being very young and a bit unsure of not being with mommy and daddy, they would fuss when Rose would put them to bed at night.

Rose would get them in the bed, lie down with them, and just start to sing over them. She would insert their names in the songs as she sang; this seemed to add to their sense of comfort and trust. Soon after this, the twins would fall asleep, safe and sound. There were many times that both Cole and Jade fell asleep while their Nana sang to them.

One night, however, something amazing happened that left an indescribable impression on Rose that would rank as one of the most precious memories of her life. This particular night, as she lay down with the kids and sang them to sleep, all of a sudden they started quietly singing back to her. Now, Nana's songs of affirmation over the grandkids caused them to sing reciprocating words of affirmation over her.

Do you get the picture here? As Daddy rejoices over us with singing and we begin to experience the peace and contentment that His love brings, our hearts cannot keep silent; we begin to rejoice over Him with singing. Now, both Father and son/daughter are caught up together as one in a harmonious melody of love. This, my dear friend, is the love song we have always longed to hear!

Chapter 14

But I've Made Such
a Mess of Things!

I n my last book, *The Offense of Grace*, I wrote about the five
faces or people represented in the story of the Prodigal Son. I
want to mention this story again in relation to the mess the
younger son had made of his life. As with so many people today, when
we look at where we have come from and where we have ended up at
times, it can be a bit disheartening.

> *"Not long after that, the younger son got together all he
> had, set off for a distant country and there squandered his
> wealth in wild living. After he had spent everything, there
> was a severe famine in that whole country, and he began
> to be in need. So he went and hired himself out to a citizen
> of that country, who sent him to his fields to feed pigs. He
> longed to fill his stomach with the pods that the pigs were
> eating, but no one gave him anything"* (Luke 15:13-16).

Does any of this story sound familiar to you? Is there any part of
these verses with which we can identify? Remember, the first step to

healing is honesty, so let's be honest. First of all, let me state that there is no condemnation intended here. The purpose is not to resurrect some old sin and restore the shame or guilt you may have felt back then. No, it is just a simple question that I think needs answering.

Perhaps as you read this, you find yourself in a similar country as this young son was; just the mention of it is stirring the saliva glands and causing your stomach to growl. Maybe, or should I say hopefully, the stench of the hog farm you have hired yourselves out to is making you nauseous enough to want to get out.

Well, if you answered in the affirmative to any of these questions, join the ranks of probably everyone around you that you have ever known. In truth, we all sin, miss the mark, fall short, and too often just make a royal mess of things. Maybe that's why the apostle John admonished/encouraged us in the following verses.

> *If we claim to be without sin, we deceive ourselves and the truth is not in us. If we confess our sins, he is faithful and just and will forgive us our sins and purify us from all unrighteousness* (1 John 1:8-9).

At this point and for our discussion, I don't really think the type of sin we committed is the main issue; neither is the effect it may have had on us, on our family, or on our world, though it most assuredly did have some effect. The bottom line is that we were in a place we should not be, with people we should never have been with, and doing things we hopefully at this point are very sorry we did! Have you come to your senses yet?

> *"When he came to his senses, he said, 'How many of my father's hired men have food to spare, and here I am starving to death! I will set out and go back to my father and say to him, father, I have sinned against heaven and against you. I am no longer worthy to be called your son; make me like one of your hired men.' So he got up and went to his father. But while he was still a long way off, his father saw*

*him and was filled with compassion for him; he ran to his
son, threw his arms around him and kissed him"*
(Luke 15:17-20).

There are a couple of things I want us to see through all of this.
First of all, and I will try to sum it up because it is not my main point,
when you are in the pig pen, not only do you stink, but so does everyone around you . . . eventually.

Back in the late '70s Rose and I for two years lived in a small, rural
Iowa town named Dows. We had a great time with great people. I had
a job delivering propane gas for the local COOP. My responsibilities
included at times going into some of the many hog confinements in
that area to attempt to fix or restart a heater. Without fail, when I got
home at the end of the day, even if I had just been in the hog pen for
a few minutes, Rose knew where I was. In fact, fortunately at the time
we lived in an old farmhouse in the country, so she would make me
strip down to my long johns before I entered the house.

Even after taking almost everything off, my hair, mustache, and
pretty much everything still smelled. To make matters worse, I would
carry the odor in the house as well. You see, when you stink, you stink.
We can splash on all the perfume in the world, but under it all you
still have stink. This is part of the problem in the "Church" today.

We use a lot of religious perfume to hide what we are really like.
We wear the finest clothes, say all the right words, go through all the
motions, and know most of the songs. We raise our hands, dance, and
shout "Hallelujah" and "Amen Preacher", but at the end of the day,
we are still carrying the fragrance from the "distant country" we so
often visit.

I think this is a much bigger problem today than we would like to
admit or to imagine, yet it is not the main focus of this book. I will
say this, however: I think the world has pretty much figured out us
Christians. From a mile away the world can recognize a hog farmer
disguised as a Christian. For some reason, people in the world have a

very sensitive sense of smell. Perhaps it is because they are so desperate to smell the fragrance of real life!

The other point I want us to see in this story is the Father's reaction to the son's return. Thankfully, his reaction is far different than most of ours when it concerns someone who has gone astray and decides to return home. It seems today that we are more "clean-up-so-you-can-get-cleaned-up" type of people.

We often insist people shed their stinky "hog-farmer clothes" before they can come into many of our high-dollar, high-profile, Hollywood-style production studios before we can accept them into our club—I mean, church. It seems like we want people to take a shower before they get a bath. It is kind of like cleaning the fish before it gets caught. How in the world does that work? (Was that politically correct? *Hmmm.*)

When this repentant, badly smelling young man finally came to his senses and started "home", his dad, who ever since the day the boy left had apparently been looking out over the horizon and hoped to see his son return, went anxiously running towards him. To the amazement of, I am sure, everyone; dad went running to the son without his bottle of disinfectant and anti-bacterial spray!

The heart of the father was beating like never before as he saw his son returning on the path to the home place. His first thoughts were not what the boy had done or where he had been or the balance in his bank account. He was simply filled with compassion; his first thought was, "My son is coming home!" Without any thought of what he, himself, is wearing or what the servants or any other onlookers might be thinking, the father embraces his son.

Wow, can you imagine that? The son insulted his dad in the first place by asking for the inheritance. Then, he broke his dad's heart by leaving home. To make matters worse, he wasted everything that dad gave him and that he had worked so hard for. We have not even gotten to the "wild living" and the prostitutes yet.

But dad, setting aside his dignity, as it were, and thinking nothing of the punishment probably due this kid, ran to him and grabbed him for one reason only—to love him. As tears from both intermingled on their cheeks that were pressed together, the father felt the joy of a returned son; the son felt forgiven—all, by the way, before the boy even actually apologized! Notice what happens next.

> *"The son said to him, 'Father, I have sinned against heaven and against you. I am no longer worthy to be called your son.' But the father said to the servants, 'Quick! Bring the best robe and put it on him. Put a ring on his finger and sandals on his feet. Bring the fattened calk and kill it. Let's have a feast and celebrate. For this son of mine was dead and is alive again, he was lost and is found.' So they began to celebrate"* (Luke 15:21-24).

Do you realize what we have just read here, and I might add experience, every time we return from this same smelly, distant country that this boy in our story did? The "best robe" in the house is placed on the dirty, smelly son as though he were royalty. Then, the best of the family jewels is placed on his finger that was mud-stained with who knows what.

And can you imagine what his feet looked like? Apparently, this didn't even matter to the dad, so on the boy's feet go what was, no doubt, a pair of his dad's sandals. Now, should you be from the "get-clean-before-you-get-clean group" or the "clean-the-fish-before-you-catch-him" crowd and cannot imagine what I have just described and think the servants may have washed him up first, then at least consider the hug he gets before anything else happened. Either way, this is almost too good to be true.

How could this all be happening to someone who has just made such a mess of things in his life? Why is it that a person who can do so much damage to his family, himself, and no doubt, to the heart of God be up for such seemingly "preferential" treatment? Could it possibly be because our loving Heavenly Father, who from time to time I affectionately call *Daddy* or *Papa*, really loves us?

Am I to dare believe that He might be more concerned for you and me as individuals than He is over the mess we have made of things? Is this the glimmer of hope we have all been looking for? Can it really be that *Yahweh*, *El Shaddai* (God Almighty), *Adonai* (Master or Lord), *El Elyon* (Most High), *Jehovah* (Lord), *Father, Daddy,* or *Papa*—whatever we choose to call Him—really loves us? Uh, yeah!

My friend, this is all true. You are loved today. The heart of God really loves you. Yes, He knew about our messes beforehand, yet He still loves us. ***All the days ordained for me were written in your book before one of them came to be*** (Ps. 139:16). And, just imagine, He still loves me. *Jesus loves me, this I know, for the Bible tells me so.* I am sorry, but all that negative stuff I have heard from some people, was wrong!

I am not going to ruin such a great discussion right now with the attitude of the "older brother" in our story who got really mad because of what the father did for "that son of his" (Luke 15:25-32) who really made a mess of things. Perhaps I will just say that I think he was very possibly a charter member of the "get-clean-before-you-get-clean" and the "clean-the-fish-before-you-catch-him" club.

More worthy and more exciting to quote, however, might be what my "Older Brother" has said. Do you mind if I close this chapter with a bit of reminiscing over a few words that He said that have, in the past, and continue even now, to help me?

> *"Come unto me, all you who are weary and burdened,*
> *and I will give you rest. Take my yoke upon you and learn*
> *from me, for I am gentle and humble in heart, and you*
> *will find rest for your souls. For my yoke is easy and my*
> *burden is light"* (Mt. 11:29-30).

Jesus straightened up and asked her, "Woman, where are they? Has no one condemned you?" "No one sir," she said. "Then neither do I condemn you," Jesus declared. "Go now and leave your life of sin" (John 8:10-11).

"For God so loved the world that he gave his one and only Son, that whosoever believes in him shall not perish but have eternal life. For God did not send his son into the world to condemn the world, but to save the world through him" (John 3:16-17).

Chapter 15

Entering His Presence

One of the benefits that I have personally experienced through this journey we have been on for the last 12 or 13 years of discovering our true identity and experiencing more of the Father's Love has been imagery. What I mean by that is being able more and more to place myself into a Bible story and with the simplicity of a child ask my Daddy what's going on. For me, I gain some amazing insight as He is simply blown away by our desire to know Him more in childlike faith.

I like to imagine what it would be like to be there in the story, if even just as an observer, and to receive a greater impact of what is really going on. What would it be like to experience what the participants experienced on that particular day? What would it be like to see a burning bush not being consumed (Ex. 3:2), the sun stand still (Josh. 10:13), a nine-foot giant fall to the ground after being hit in the forehead with one small rock (1 Sam. 17:40-49), or a widow's jar not running out of oil? (2 Kings 4:1-7).

When the angel Gabriel told Mary she would carry a child from God (Luke 1:26-35) and the angel of the Lord confirms to Joseph in a dream that this really was from God (Mt. 1:19-25), how would that have felt? Can you imagine what it would be like to experience a chorus of angels all of a sudden surrounding your sheep herd and starting to sing what, at least to you, would have been a new song? (Luke 2:8-14).

Now I don't know about you, but watching five small loaves of bread and two small fish feed more than 5,000 men, besides women and children, would be an amazing sight (Mark 6:38-44)—not to mention watching Lazarus, after being dead for several days, hopping out of his tomb as he is bound hand and foot (John 11:34-44) or seeing blind eyes opened and deaf ears hearing (Mt. 11:5). And how priceless it would be to watch Jesus silence a room full of skeptics (Luke 2:42-47).

Well, besides Jesus, of course, my favorite Bible character would be Moses. I really don't know what exactly it was that made him my favorite, but ever since I can remember—since I was a baby Christian—Moses seems to have been the one that really has moved my heart. Here you have an amazing man with an amazing gift to be able to speak to God "mouth to mouth", not to mention his ability to lead a tremendous nation out of bondage. It just doesn't get any better than that!

I suppose like me there are some questions you would love to ask many of these Bible characters that we have come to know like family. Well, if I could sit with Moses for a few minutes and talk with him, there would be many things I would love to hear his personal take on. There is one question I would ask. Many think I am kidding about this, but it really intrigues me. OK, so now you are going to know how simple-minded I really am.

I really want to ask Moses about what it was like when he and the children of Israel journeyed through the Red Sea shortly after they left Egypt (Ex. 14:15-22). Now if I were like some of the skeptics today who say that the water was at a low point at that time and likely only a couple of inches deep, then of course my question would be, how in the world did two-inch-deep water drown so many of the men in Pharaoh's army? (Ex. 14:23-28).

But no, here is my genuine and most sincere question for Moses. "Moses, when you led all of the people through the Red Sea on 'dry ground' . . . (here it is) . . . could you see the fish?" I mean, come on, haven't you ever thought about that yourself? Were the people, as they looked to the right or left at the wall of water on either side, staring at the fish and watching as the fish stared back at them? You have to wonder what both people and fish were thinking! Don't you?

Well, there is so much imagery in the Bible, which, while not coming right out and saying some things, speaks volumes about an issue. The Book of Esther and the Tabernacle in the Wilderness are just two of those stories that speak volumes to us about God, life, and the pursuit of true happiness. I want to take a look at these two visual teachers and learn what we can about entering His presence.

There is so much about Esther that I want to say. I will get to it in just a little bit, but there is someone that I want to look at that I don't hear a lot about. Since I am not really trying to present a theological thesis here on the subject, please allow me to take the liberty of making some comparison and analogy in the rest of this chapter.

I have never really read much about the first queen in the Book of Esther—Queen Vashti. There are several differing thoughts as to why she refused to come before the king when he summoned her that day (Esth. 1:10-12). Many commentators suggest, and maybe rightly so, that Queen Vashti's disobedience was a courageous act of humility and dignity worthy of praise. For whatever reason she chose to disobey, she would have known it would cost her the crown!

What if Queen Vashti represents many of us? The king had just spent the better part of six months throwing the biggest party that perhaps the world had ever seen up to that point. Even the Queen threw her own banquet for her peers. So at this point, everyone seems happy, well-fed, and in high spirits. Seemingly nothing could ruin this festive mood—that is until the king summons you to his palace to display your beauty to the world! Then all of a sudden, you begin to have second thoughts about his motives, his expectations, and the ultimate cost to you. Sound familiar? I am reminded here of another King who has a much more beautiful Bride/Queen and who is capable of throwing a celebration far greater than that of Ling Xerxes.

> *"In the same way, I tell you (and He should know), there is rejoicing in the presence of the angels of God over one sinner who repents"* (Luke 15:10).

When we first came to Christ, at least for many of us, there was much talk about the freedom, favor, and fun that was now ours as members of the Kingdom of God. I mean come on: we were promised the Holy Spirit, who would come and bestow upon us unbelievable gifts, power, and authority.

For most of us, coming from the life of a mere peasant, this was all more than we could ever hope for or imagine. So, we came along for the ride of a lifetime and even had hopes of a life after this one that was unexplainable . . . *No eye has seen, no ear has heard, no mind has conceived what God has prepared for those who love him* (1 Cor. 2:9).

So far so good—that is, until we are summoned before the King and find that the displaying of our beauty might mean trials, temptations, and even some suffering. Now, we begin to have second thoughts and deny His request to appear. Remember, up to now, there would have been few if any reasons why the Queen would not have considered it an honor and privilege to come before the king or show off her beauty.

When have you ever known a Bride that was not at least a little excited and proud at the way she looked on that special day? But how many of those Brides would be so happy and excited if they knew the next step of their new journey might lead to tears, trouble, and tur-moil? Not many, I suppose.

I believe we are much more like Queen Vashti than we would like to think. Many of us have gotten so caught up in our new freedom, favor, and fun that we don't have the time or desire to run off to the King and "show off" our beauty. I mean, really: I am enjoying these "gifts" and all the "attention" I am getting right here. What could possibly be better than this?

No matter how you look at it, Queen Vashti's refusal to go before the king that day revealed either her own selfishness, her outright dis-obedience, or "her" interpretation of the motives of the king. Whatever her reasoning, she decided to deny his request. Her lack of submission might be an indication of the lack of "knowledge" and "trust" she had in her husband, the king. Maybe she had cause for this, but we don't!

What if our King summons us solely for the purpose of showing us off to the world as a testimony to His glory, as He did with Pharaoh? *For the Scripture says to Pharaoh: "I raised you up for this very purpose, that I might display my power in you and that my name might be proclaimed in all the earth"* (Rom. 9:17).

Listen to how Paul refers to himself and other apostles. *For it seems to me that God has put us apostles on display at the end of the procession, like men condemned to die in the arena. We have been made a spectacle to the whole universe, to angels as well as to men. We are fools for Christ, but you are so wise in Christ! We are weak, but you are strong! You are honored, we are dishonored!* (1 Cor. 4:9-10).

It would appear from what Jesus said that the only way we can re-ally live is to die to our own wants and desires. So, if He wants us to give up our pride, our goals, and our desires for Him, so be it. *"Whoever finds his life will lose it, and whoever loses his life for my sake will find it"* (Mt. 11:39). But, if we willingly give it all up for Him, the payback is amazing, albeit there may be some persecution (Mk. 10:29-34).

Let's move to another Queen now; her name is Esther. She is Vashti's replacement, as it were; the story of her rise to the place of power and prominence is not only amazing, but it is a blueprint for entering the presence of our King and living in intimacy with Him and His Father. We can learn much from this orphan girl-turned-Queen on how to captivate the heart of a King and to enjoy favor few have ever enjoyed.

We know that Queen Vashti was removed from her place as Queen after her refusal to obey the order of the king when he summoned her to display her beauty. So, after checking with his officials as to what should be done, the suggestion was made for the king to order that a search be made throughout his kingdom to find a suitable replacement.

As you can imagine, this would not be just any replacement; she would have to be near perfect in meeting all of the king's expectations. Not only would this new woman be Queen, she would be one who by her beauty and status would somehow represent the king's wisdom, power, and authority. Finding one suitable for this task would not be easy.

So, a search is made throughout all 127 provinces in the kingdom. Based on some historical speculation, there would have been more than 400 women chosen as candidates. Being chosen as one of these women, in and of itself, would have been a tremendous honor. Most of these women would not have come from a comfortable lifestyle, so for them, it would have been an amazing promotion.

Not unlike us, when you really think about where we came from before we accepted Christ and became citizens of this new kingdom in which we are now soujourners, the comparison between the two worlds is nothing short of amazing. Through Christ, we received the biggest promotion possible in all of human history!

To get ready for what might be their one-night opportunity to gain the favor of the king, these 400-plus women had to undergo 12 months of preparation inside and out. During this time, the privilege of the kingdom would have been theirs. Being treated as royalty, these women would have enjoyed the best clothes, jewelry, and food the kingdom could offer.

With all of these beautiful women to choose from, how in the world would the king be able to make the right choice for the next Queen? I mean, imagine this: You have 400 of the most beautiful women in the whole kingdom, all of which have undergone deep, detailed beauty treatments. All were dressed in the best money could afford. The air must have been intoxicating with the fragrance of the best perfumes in the world. It must have been blinding to see all these beauties wearing beautiful and, I might add, expensive jewelry.

How do you make that one right choice when there is so much of the same to choose from? What could possibly be the deciding factor in the heart of the king to make him choose just one to be his Queen? It is kind of like trying to buy a gift for the person who has everything. What is that one thing that would really, if possible, bring out the joy and excitement that that gift was meant to bring?

Consider this also. It has been suggested that these women would have been able to keep for life all of the clothes and all of the jewelry they received while in this beauty contest. Not to mention that for the rest of their lives they would have received both special treatment and amazing favor. So for them, all they had to do was walk the walk and talk the talk and they were in, so to speak.

This means that even if they didn't get chosen as that special one to be Queen, they still had it made. I suppose then that for some of these women, just getting by would have been good enough. Thinking more of themselves perhaps and the privilege they now enjoyed, it would be easy to conceal what was really in their hearts for that one night with the king.

So again, with more than 400 of the most beautiful women in the world to choose from—all looking pretty much alike and all saying just the right things—how do you get to be that special one? It helps if you know the heart of the king. And at this time, nobody knows the heart of the king—that is, knows everything about him and his likes and dislikes—except one man: Hegai, the man entrusted with the care of the king's harem.

This man was not some favored babysitter watching over the king's girls. This man had this position because he knew the king's heart. He knew the king's heart because he would have had access to the inner chambers of the king's life. In the kingdom, there were several different layers of access designed to limit the people who got close to the king.

The closer you got to the king himself, the tougher the security and the fewer the people who were allowed to enter. Hegai would have been considered a "chamberlain" or basically, someone who had access to the inner chambers of the king's life. He would have seen and heard things about the king that few ever did. No doubt, there were many personal talks between him and the king.

One thing is for sure: his privilege would have taught him the king's heart. So, when one of the women in his charge was summoned to the bedchamber of the king, Hegai would be able to tell beforehand if she would make it or not. Why? Because he, himself, knew the king intimately.

So when it came time for Esther to get ready for her night with the king, she submitted to this chamberlain for his wisdom on what would please the king. ***When it came time for Esther . . . she asked for nothing other than what Hegai, the king's eunuch who was in charge of the harem, suggested. And Esther won the favor of everyone who saw her*** (Esth. 2:15).

Having the choice of the best of the best in the entire kingdom, this soon-to-be queen listened only to what the chamberlain, arguably the one who knew the king better than anyone, suggested. Did she have natural beauty? Of course, but then so did the 400 other women. But when given the choice of wearing what she thought would make her beautiful, she listened to the man who knew the beauty the king longed for.

Esther chose the king over his kingdom. She sought after the person more than she did the privilege. Her greatest desire was relationship, not rewards. And the truth is, when she made these decisions, not only did she win the heart of the king, but she got the kingdom, the privilege, and the rewards anyway!

Those who would enter the presence of the Father to know and experience His amazing love would do best to enter with one thing in mind—Him and Him alone! When it is our heart to know His heart and to bring joy and pleasure to Him, His heart is captivated by our love. There are so many who look the same, smell the same, and talk the same, but He is looking for those who can find their rest, reward, and peace in Him.

> *He who dwells in the shelter of the Most High will rest in the shadow of the Almighty. I will say of the Lord, "He is my refuge and my fortress, my God in whom I trust"* (Ps. 91:1-2).

He is looking for those who will come before Him and stay a while and not run by for a quick pit stop. He longs for those who want Him more than they want what He can give or do for them. As a Father, I believe He enjoys those who will look to Him as their protector, provider, and source of eternal pleasure.

My friend, I encourage you to be like Esther, who had one thing in mind—that was the king. When we lay ourselves down for Him, submitting to the leadership and wisdom of the Holy Spirit, the One who knows His heart like no other, we set ourselves on a course of intimacy and favor that we cannot imagine.

When we come to Him as little children that stare up into His eyes with that look of desire, dependence, and delight, His heart is moved. He has room in His Heart for all of us. When He sees us coming toward Him from off in the distance, I assure you He runs toward us with open arms. The first thing we feel is His arms around us (His intimate presence); then come the robe, the ring, and the sandals (things).

Lay this book down right now and just talk to Him. Tell Him how much you love Him and long to know Him more intimately. If you have to, ask Him to forgive you for being more enamored with the kingdom than the King. Tell Him how you now desire Him more than you desire the privilege of being a son or daughter. Whisper in His ear how much more you want relationship than rewards.

When you do—and when it comes from a heart of sincerity and desperation—I promise you His Heart is moved toward yours. The results are yet to be discovered!

Chapter 16

Going Deeper

There is yet another picture I see in Scripture that floods my heart with imagery when it comes to going deeper into the Heart of the Father. For me, it reveals some potential layers of access available to all of us. Sadly, I think, few recognize the need or value of going deeper. Perhaps many do desire a closer relationship and intimacy with the Father but may not understand that it is possible or how to facilitate it! I want us to look briefly at the Tabernacle in the Wilderness.

From the Book of Exodus, chapters 25-40, we can learn much about the initial call of God to Moses to make this Tabernacle and the details about its furnishings and purpose. The description of this new project ends with the following information, instruction, and promise:

> *Then the cloud covered the Tent of Meeting, and the glory of the Lord filled the tabernacle. Moses could not enter the Tent of Meeting because the cloud had settled upon it, and*

*the glory of the Lord filled the tabernacle. In all the travels
of the Israelites whenever the cloud lifted from above the
tabernacle, they would set out; but if the cloud did not lift,
they did not set out—until the day it lifted. So the cloud of
the Lord was over the tabernacle by day, and the fire was
in the cloud by night, in the sight of all the house of Israel
during their travels* (Ex. 40:34-38).

The Tabernacle in the Wilderness

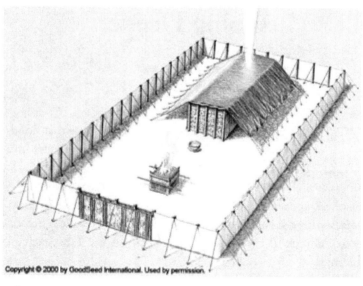

Image from http://www.the-tabernacle-place.com/tabernacle_articles/tabernacle_basic_layout.aspx

When you glance at the drawing of the Tabernacle, it reveals what
I see as three levels of intimacy with God. Remember, I am using imagery here and not trying to post a theological statement based on what
you might read in a set of commentaries on the chapters in Exodus.

What are we willing to pay, if necessary, for the deepest level of intimacy possible with the Father on this side of eternity?

I also want to make it clear here that there is no condemnation implied at all to those who are comfortable with where they are at right now with God. Going deeper, I believe, is God's hope and desire for all of us, but I think He really leaves it up to us to decide how deep we want to go. In other words, if you or I choose to stay where we are as far as our depth with Daddy is concerned, He will not throw any lightning bolts our way to get us moving closer. Or, maybe He will . . ..

This whole idea of throwing darts and condemnation on people is really a problem in the "Church" today. Imagine how this might really look from the outside. We try to draw people into the Kingdom of God by threatening them with hell fire and doom and gloom. We show them a picture of an angry, short-fused God who can't wait to send them to hell. (I do admit that there are times when strong language with some people is probably necessary.)

Then once they are "in", we weigh them down with a set of rules and regulations that most people can't keep up with, let alone follow and observe. We warn them again of this angry God's quick temper and admonish them to walk on tippy toes throughout the rest of their lives in hopes of not setting Him off. Oh, and by the way, the Father really loves you and wants to spend eternity with you!

Could this be one of the reasons why much of the "Church" today is ineffective when it comes to displaying the power and glory of God? Have we gotten people so afraid of a God of which they have no real understanding that they would rather hide their talents in the ground than put them to work for His glory? (Mt. 25:14-30).

I have heard that every week in this country there are thousands of people who walk away from Evangelical churches and never return to a church of any kind. I do not presume to have the answers for this, but I do have a thought on the matter. Could it be that people who don't really have an understanding of the Father's love—who have tried

and tried to "make it work" as a Christian, yet continue to fall short—
finally give up?

Has the image of a loving, caring, and compassionate God been
so distorted to us that many simply walk away in shame and disgust
and believe they have never been and never will be good enough for
Him? Is the "Church" today somehow guilty of causing thousands of
spiritual abortions every day around this world?

Has all of "our" pushing, shoving, and hammering people over the
head with the Big Family Bible finally taken its toll on the "baby"
Christians? Has the lying, screaming, fighting, and discord that is all
too common within so many of our churches today caused such
trauma to the infant Christians, still not fully developed, to be forced
out of the nurturing womb, so to speak, before they can survive on
their own? It is amazing to me how we can point out all the wrongs in
this world around us and yet never look within our own hearts! Well,
I digress.

In the drawing of the Tabernacle in the Wilderness you will notice
the large courtyard surrounding the Tent of Meeting. This courtyard
was considered a meeting place between God and the Israelites and
would have been entered by many people who would, after meeting
the requirements of entrance, enjoy the benefit of being inside. They
would have enjoyed a measure of protection and privilege that came
with being there.

Yes, the Brazen Altar and Laver (Basin) are there as well, but they
serve as a reminder of the price someone (Jesus) paid for us to enter
this place and the need to daily cleanse oneself. You see, even though
we are "in", there are times when we need to wash ourselves from the
daily grime of life.

> *If we claim to be without sin, we deceive ourselves and the
> truth is not in us. If we confess our sins, he is faithful and
> just and will forgive us our sins and purify us from all un-
> righteousness. If we claim we have not sinned, we make
> him out to be a liar and his word has no place in our lives*
> (1 John 1:8-10).

So, being a citizen of the courtyard would be great. There would be lots of fellowship, implied protection, and the assurance of knowing you were a part of something much bigger than yourself. You could roam around, for the most part, freely and enjoy the fruits of citizenship. Who could ask for any more than that? Well, not many do, but there are those who are curious about the Tent in the middle of the courtyard.

To me, the courtyard represents "average" Christian living, if there is such a thing. Because of our being "in", we are often low-impact, low-energy, and low-motivation type of folks. We found Christ one day and know we are headed to heaven (or at least we hope), so let's grin and bear it until we get there. Well, that is one attitude people can have, but let me ask you this:

Doesn't the fact that there is a Tent right here in the middle of our courtyard that appears to have a cloud of smoke rising from it make you at least a little curious? I mean after all, when we are driving down the road and see off in the distance a cloud of smoke, most of us will slow down and will stretch our necks to see what is burning. Why not here in the courtyard? I wonder if the lives of those around us who claim to be from this tent keep us from wanting anything to do with it.

When we look at this Tent, we begin to realize that within it are two separate and distinct rooms. The first is larger than the second, but the second room—the smaller one—seems to be where there is the greatest mystery. Let's look at this larger room first. Somehow, being in this room seems a little more personal and intimate than the courtyard does. For some, at least, there is an inner drawing to be inside here.

This room would have been entered daily as the priests would enter to take care of the furniture inside and to see to it that the light and remembrance never dimmed in the hearts of the people. In this room as you entered were three pieces of furniture, as near as I can tell.

First to be noticed when you entered would be the Golden Candlesticks on your immediate left.

Then to your immediate right there was a Table of Showbread with fresh-baked loaves of bread on it, no doubt illuminated by the light of the Candles. Then in the center of the room was what was called the Altar of Incense. Every day, the Priests would enter this place and make sure the candles were supplied with the oil that was required to keep them burning.

They also daily would make sure there were fresh loaves of bread placed on the Table and that the incense never ran out. So, it is safe to assume that far fewer people entered this place than were allowed in the courtyard. To be one of the priests that served in this first room, called "The Holy Place", would have been a tremendous honor and privilege. They were specially chosen for this sacred task.

You and I have the freedom to enter deeper as well. In the Holy Place the candles could represent the Holy Spirit and the Table of Bread could represent fellowship with Christ, the Bread of Life. So, in this place, for the "chosen"—that is, for "whosoever will"—we can come and enjoy the light and warmth of the Precious Holy Spirit and enjoy intimate fellowship with Jesus.

Imagine this intimate interaction with the very Breath and Bread of God. In this place, away from the crowd, away from the noise and distractions of the outside world, we can come to simply know Him. Here, we find no pressure, false expectations, or pressure to perform. Now, alone with Him, you can really discover more about who He is and, I might add, who you are.

Maybe the Altar of Incense represents that place where you and I can lay ourselves down under the close, comforting care of a Loving God. It is a place of unbelievable warmth and fellowship where those things that may hinder us fall or burn away. As the Sacrifice in heaven meets with one of His children and the light of His Presence burns away at the things of the world still lingering in us, to the Nostrils of the Father a fragrance rises which brings Him great pleasure.

This second level of access, if you will, brings us a greater sense of value, contentment, and purpose. As I said earlier, we begin to see Him much more closely; our level of understanding of the love He really has for us is illuminated. Our thoughts become less and less about ourselves and more and more about Him. Maybe, for the first time ever, we can see Him as Daddy!

Now this Holy Place is a place I think I could enjoy forever. In it we are surrounded by the very heartbeat of the Father. With little or no concern for ourselves, we can begin to enjoy things we previously thought were unobtainable. It is not necessarily that being in this room alone with God makes you more special than those lingering in the courtyard, but because this room is special, it makes you want to leave the courtyard and enter in!

Finally, as we enjoy the presence of God in this Holy Place, our eyes can't help but be drawn to yet another room. It seems like there is still a deeper level of access ahead of us. The longer we rest in this room (Holy Place) the more we desire to be in that room (Most Holy Place). There is something tugging at our hearts and we hear a whisper in our ears saying, "Come closer still!" Is it possible? Could there be more? Ah, we will see.

This final room has a strange, yet curious, entrance. Clearly there was a curtain of sorts that separated these two rooms, but now the curtain seems to have been hastily and violently torn apart. Our sense is that someone—apparently someone extremely strong and no doubt desperate—was making it possible for you and me to enter this room.

Previously, in the actual Tabernacle that Moses built and that was carried through the wilderness, only one person came into this final room—and even then, only once a year. In the past, the total number of priests that would have entered here would be very small. So this exhilaration that we feel right now must be because we know we are going somewhere few have ever gone. Yet, it is now available to all.

Apparently, the tear in this curtain resembles two other tears we have seen before in Scripture. *He parted the heavens and came down;*

dark clouds were under his feet (Ps. 18:9). *As Jesus was coming up out of the water, he saw heaven being torn open . . .* (Mk. 1:10). The first tear occurred when the Father was coming to deliver His servant, David. The second tear happened as the Father was coming to see His Son, Jesus.

This now before us seems to be a third tearing away. *At that moment the curtain of the temple was torn in two from top to bottom. The earth shook and the rocks split* (Mt. 27:51). This time, the tearing away is for us. Now, you and I have access into this deeper level—this place of unspeakable intimacy.

> *"I am the way and the truth and the life. No one comes to the Father except through me. If you really knew me, you would know my Father as well. From now on, you do know him and have seen him"* (John 14:6-7).

As soon as Jesus died on that Cross those many years ago, the curtain that kept us from this room was torn apart to perhaps fulfill what we just read in John's Gospel. His obedience in every way to His Father while He walked this earth, culminating with His death on that old rugged cross, became our point of entrance. Jesus is the pathway we have to travel, but the destination has always been the Father.

This doesn't mean we are done with Jesus now, God forbid! No, He not only is our Lord and Savior, the King of Kings, and the Lord of Lords, but He is also our Bridegroom. For all eternity we will be in the presence of our Lord and His Father. What this does mean, however, is that now—yes, right now—we can enter into the next level of access.

As I said earlier, when Jesus died for us it was not, as far too many believe today, just for our "get-out-of-hell" free pass. No, while that is certainly a side benefit of the whole process, the main goal was to make a way for the Father to come to us and enjoy again the sweet fellowship He lost after the fall in the Garden. It would do us well to consider more often what the Father is feeling and needing rather than always making life about us! Yes, because of the fall, man lost fellowship with God, but He also lost that intimacy with us. Since intimacy with Man was His greatest desire, maybe His loss was greater than ours.

The Holy Place may be the preparation place for getting us ready to enter the Most Holy Place. Now, we are prepared and ready to come to the Throne of Grace and Mercy and sit at the feet of our Daddy. All alone in this place, it is just Him and us. Nothing else matters, and it is here we begin to experience the fullness of His love (Ps. 91:1).

When the Father breathed life into the nostrils of Adam (Gen. 2:7), an act that would have so much resembled a kiss, it gave instant life to the Man. At that moment—that exact moment when life entered Adam—what would he have seen? He would have been looking into the eyes of his Creator, his God, but more importantly, his Daddy.

For Adam, before words were ever spoken between him and the Father, he would have known beyond any shadow of doubt that his Daddy would take care of every need he might ever have. He would have known the fullness of peace and the unlimited power of love. For Adam, this would have been life, and that, more abundantly! (John 10:10b).

My friend, I fear that precious few have dared to pursue this level of intimacy with the Father, perhaps believing it unobtainable. Whether it be because of a lack of knowledge, a lingering sense of failure and unworthiness, or simply an unwillingness to relinquish the "rights" to ourselves to this most awesome, loving Father, few have sought access.

Here is the good news for all of us: you can come to this place. It is available to all of us, regardless of the debris left in our past or the masked aroma of our present. I will even be so bold as to say that "This is why you and I were created!" We were made by Love, for love, so that we, too, might love in return.

One of them, an expert in the law, tested him with this question: "Teacher, which is the greatest commandment in the Law?" Jesus replied: "Love the Lord your God with all

> *your heart and with all your soul and with all your mind.*
> *This is the first and greatest commandment. And the*
> *second is like it: Love your neighbor as yourself. All the*
> *Law and the Prophets hang on these two commandments"*
> (Mt. 22:35-40).

There is such simplicity offered by Jesus here in response to the question posed Him by this Pharisee, an "expert" in the Law. I have said it before, but it warrants repeating again right here. Very simply, love God and love man. That's it. It sums up just about everything in life and if followed will prevent most sins and years of heartache. Oh yes, there will still be trials and challenges, but if we follow these two commands, somehow everything will be alright!

I know that right about now someone must be thinking that all this "love stuff" can be carried a bit too far. I mean after all, "We can't overlook people's sins" and "What if they . . .?" Thoughts of "sloppy *agape*" begin to swirl around in our minds as we think about all of this. That inner voice of "maturity" is trying to break in and bring us back to reality.

In two separate instances I was questioned about this very thing while I was on a trip to Korea. In both instances some terrible sin was mentioned; then my friends were trying to get me to see that what the "sinner" in these situations needed was not love but severe punishment. With the greatest of sincerity, they presented their case to me by saying that "these people didn't deserve grace." Rather, due to the horrendous nature of their sin, they deserved "justice"!

I have to be honest with you: When I hear people throw around the "J" word like that, it scares me, because I don't think they realize what they are really saying or demanding. My understanding is that the word *justice* means "fair" or "getting what one deserves". I fully agree with there being severe consequences for some bad things that are done. No problem with that at all.

Where I do tremble a little is when I realize that when I begin to demand *"justice"* toward other people who do wrong, I am at the same

176

time demanding it for myself. And believe me, brother: I do not want to get what I deserve. I'll stick with the "grace" crowd and trust God to sort it all out.

Another issue raised when I talk about this love is this: People say that all this talk about love can become for some a license to sin more. Good point, but I think we are overlooking one thing: When we really discover true love from our Heavenly Father, we will live a life free from anything that will jeopardize this love.

Let's get back to the Most Holy Place. I can't promise you what things will be whispered to you in this secret place. I don't know what revelations you might be given or the responsibilities and challenges you may be called to walk through in your life. But one thing I do know is that regardless of what you hear or what you might be compelled to do, there will be unprecedented peace and assurance like you have never experienced before in your life.

Conclusion

As I sit here and think of how I am going to end this book and what, if anything else, I can say that I haven't already, I have come to the realization that all that I know about the love and tenderness of God, every intimate experience I have enjoyed over these last several years, and all of the opportunities He has given Rose and me to "teach, preach, and demonstrate" His love represents only a small beginning.

By no means am I trying to suggest that I am way ahead of anyone reading this book when it comes to the experiential knowledge of Daddy's love. No, in fact, I am a bit saddened when I think of what I am still missing. My only solace in all of this is in knowing that as long as I have breath, I can still move closer. When my last breath comes, I will be there in the fullness of this amazing love!

I have tried to present in this book the true experiences of my life as I remembered them, the effect these experiences have had on me, and unfortunately that they had on many around me (Heb. 12:14-15). I think it is important to say yet again that I have meant no disrespect or harm to anyone I have mentioned but can truly thank God for each one as each has had such a profound effect on my life and helped me to get to the point I am today.

I have to be honest with you and tell you that there are still times when I do not feel like I am in the Holy Place as I sometimes still struggle with life and even question my place in the Court Yard. Oh, I know I'm in, but it sure doesn't feel like it at times. Sometimes there are just too many people in here with me.

Turning back is not an option. I really want you to say and feel the same way too. In John 6, after Jesus said to the "crowd" that was following Him some things that they just could not grasp, He then questioned them about their motives for following Him. We read the following:

> *On hearing it, many of his disciples said, "This is a hard teaching. Who can accept it?" . . . From this time many of his disciples turned back and no longer followed him* (John 6:60, 66).

Without apparently even missing a beat, Jesus looks right at the twelve and said, *"You do not want to leave too, do you?"* (vs. 67). It was then that Peter uttered the words that I have at least felt in my spirit so many times in the last 36 years of being a Christian. *"Lord, to whom shall we go? You have the words of eternal life"* (vs. 68).

My point is this: we cannot turn back, because if we allow ourselves to remember truthfully, "back there" wasn't too good. In fact, I seem to remember there being hopelessness without any hope, fear without any faith, frustration without any freedom, and hurting without any healing! So again, it wasn't that good then; what would make us think it has changed?

No, beloved, we will go forward together. Yes, there will be potholes in the middle of the road of life; yes, there will be some flat tires. But, we have the "real" AAA on our side. That is, the **Almighty: Always and Absolutely**. There is no need to dial 911, a simple *"help"* will do. You can be assured that whatever the cost, the bill will come back and say, "Paid in full at the cross!" When there seems to be no way and everything appears like a lie and life just doesn't seem to be worth it, remember, He is *"the way and the truth and the life!"*

Daddy loves you, my friend. His thoughts are not consumed with all of the problems and complexities of this world, but they rest solely on you. Sometimes, when the going gets tough, we forget what it was that got us going in the first place. It is at times like these that we need to go back to the ancient wells, or let me just say, back to the basics of our faith, and remember His Word. Let me help you with a few powerful thoughts, if I may:

> *He tends his flock like a shepherd: He gathers the lambs in his arms and caries them close to his heart; he gently leads those that have young* (Isa. 40:11).

> *But now, this is what the Lord says—He who created you, O Jacob (you and me), he who formed you, O Israel: "Fear not, for I have redeemed you; I have summoned you by name, you are mine"* (Isa. 43:1).

> *"Can a mother forget the baby at her breast and have no compassion on the child she has borne? Though she may forget, I will not forget you! See, I have engraved you on the palms of my hands; your walls are ever before me"* (Isa. 49:15-16).

> *"Though the mountains be shaken and the hills be removed, yet my unfailing love for you will not be shaken nor my covenant of peace be removed, says the Lord, who has compassion on you . . . no weapon forged against you will prevail, and you will refute every tongue that accuses you. This is the heritage of the servants of the Lord, and this is their vindication from me, declares the Lord"* (Isa. 54:10, 17).

The Lord your God is with you, he is mighty to save. He will take great delight in you, he will quiet you with his love, he will rejoice over you with singing (Zeph. 3:17).

For we are God's workmanship, created in Christ Jesus to do good works, which God prepared in advance for us to do (Eph. 2:10).

In the midst of whatever you may be going through in life right now, you can rest assured of this: Daddy is right there with you; He has a big pair of arms reaching out to you for you to jump into. Somehow, we need to get beyond the thinking that every "bad thing" that happens to us in our lives is His punishment towards us, or at best, His frustration with our apparent slowness to maturity.

I believe that it is because of the intensity of the "birth pains" (Rom. 8:18-25) today that the Father has escalated the revelation and understanding—and thus His imparting—of His tremendous love for us in these days. It is no accident that people like Jack Winter, Floyd McClung, John and Carol Arnott, and others mentioned in this book have been used as torchbearers in our generation to reveal this truth to the world.

We cannot allow the pain of our past to keep us from the potential of our future. For way too long many of us have tried to move forward while still looking in the rear view mirror. The inevitable results of that scenario are that we will crash and burn. While trying to lick our wounds from yesterday, we are being scratched and torn more and more today, to the point that so many have given up the fight.

It is almost impossible to carry all of the luggage we have accumulated from the past, add it to the baggage we may be accumulating right now, and have any hopes of walking into tomorrow. The weight will be too heavy to carry.

In our efforts to give the appearance of strength, power, and faith, many have been crushed under the enormous weight of their circumstances. Who was it that made us think we had to be strong anyway? Oh yeah, I know the cliché used so often at this point; I have unfortunately used it myself on others in the past. Are you ready to hear it again? Here it goes. *"What are you doing under your circumstances?"*

It sounds so spiritual now that I hear it again, but frankly, it seems so empty and void of help and encouragement to those being crushed. ***A cheerful heart is good medicine, but a crushed spirit dries up the bones. A man's spirit sustains him in sickness, but a crushed spirit who can bear?*** (Prov. 17:22 and 18:14).

Life is a journey. As in any journey, having someone to walk with, hold our hand, talk to, and comfort us when the going gets tough is very important. It is easy sometimes to get going but then along the way somehow to forget where you are headed. In an effort to "correct" when we get a little off-track, we sometimes overcompensate. The results can be tragic.

This book has been about my journey—the good and the bad— and how finding my true identity, has saved my life. For far too long many of us have tried to be all things to all people. If we are honest, we can say that it has almost destroyed us. After many years of being tossed around like that little metal ball in a pinball machine, we have found ourselves confused and disoriented.

The one thing that can save us from a life lived unhappy, frustrated, and seemingly without purpose is coming to the experiential reality of our true identity. That is: We are sons and daughters of Almighty God. In short, you are Daddy's little boy or girl!

Without any hesitation, I can loudly proclaim from the housetops that my life was saved when the Father used people like Jack and Trisha Frost, James and Denise Jordan, and Jack and Dorothy Winter to become an extension of this love to me. By example they "showed me" how to cultivate this relationship for myself. Rose and I are eternally thankful to the Father for bringing these people into our lives.

Now, my friend, what about you? It is your turn to receive, to be encouraged, and to be set free from the discouragement and dis-ease you have been experiencing in your life thus far. As Jack Frost used to say, it is time to stop being humans-doing and to become humans-being—being all that God intended. This is your day. You might ask, "What do I need to do?" You may not like my answer, but it is true. Absolutely nothing!

You cannot earn sonship. I had nothing to do with my natural birth; neither did you. The moment you were conceived, you "became". And what you "became" was not a doctor, lawyer, preacher, or whatever else you may "do" with your life, but you "became" a son or a daughter. That was, is, and will always be your true identity . . . DLB or DLG. Enjoy!

Other books by
Vince Mercardante Sr.

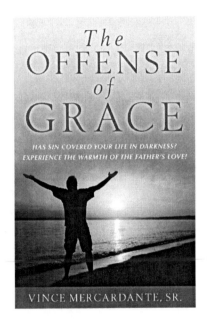

The Offense of Grace
ISBN: 978-1-934749-01-2
Retail Price: $14.95

Has sin covered your life in darkness? Experience the warmth of the Father's love!

Jesus' ministry had been well established by the time He made a trip back to His hometown. But rather than welcome back their native son as the savior He was, the town noted only the return of the carpenter's son-just another hometown boy. The price of their prejudice? They experienced few of the wonders that Jesus had performed so freely in the cities and streets of strangers. Those who should have known Jesus best could not fathom Father God working so divinely through someone they saw as all too human.

Today how many others have been overlooked because of the same kind of prejudice? Are you one who took a wrong turn, revealing your own all-too-human side? Are you now wondering whether your Father can ever use you again? Are you asking yourself how you can face those you hurt? Or how you can respond to those who still accuse you? Do you wonder how you can serve as an instrument of God when you can't even seem to shovel through your own wracking guilt?

The Offense of Grace has the answers. In loving, no-nonsense language, author Vince Mercardante acknowledges the cost of sin, but then coaches you on how to get back on track. Why sit on the sidelines, Mercardante asks—especially when you have a Father whose redemptive power can transform tragic missteps into victory laps!

The Plan of Salvation

1. The Bible says that you are accountable for the sin in your life. "For all have sinned and fall short of the glory of God" Romans 3:23.

2. A penalty exists for that sin. "For the wages of sin is death" Romans 6:23.

3. You cannot earn, by good deeds, a way to wipe out that sin from your life. "For it is by grace you have been saved, through faith-and this not from yourselves; it it the gift of God-not by works, so that no one can boast" Ephesians 2:8-9.

4. God provided for your sin by sending His Son to die in your place. Instead of you, Jesus took the wages of sin on Himself by dying on the cross. Then God raised Him on the third day. "But God demonstrates his own love for us in this: While we were still sinners, Christ died for us" Romans 5:8.

5. How do you claim this free gift of Salvation that God has provided? "Everyone who calls on the name of the Lord will be saved" Romans 10:13.

If this makes sense to you then you may pray a prayer similar to this:

"Dear God, Thank You for going to the cross for me. I believe You did it because I am a sinner and You wanted to spend eternity with me. Thank You for forgiving me of my sins and giving me a new life. I desire to change my ways and seek a relationship with You. Amen"

Now find a pastor or a Christian friend and tell him or her about your decision.

CPSIA information can be obtained at www.ICGtesting.com
Printed in the USA
LVOW102019181011

251010LV00001B/2/P